FINANCIAL SECTOR OF THE AMERICAN ECONOMY

D0169072

edited by

STUART BRUCHEY
ALLAN NEVINS PROFESSOR EMERITUS
COLUMBIA UNIVERSITY

A GARLAND SERIES

THE TRANSFORMATION OF COMMERCIAL BANKING IN THE UNITED STATES, 1956–1991

JAMES ELIOT MASON

GARLAND PUBLISHING, Inc.
A MEMBER OF THE TAYLOR & FRANCIS GROUP
NEW YORK & LONDON / 1997

Library of Congress Cataloging-in-Publication Data

Mason, James Eliot, 1951–
    The transformation of commercial banking in the United
States, 1956–1991 / James Eliot Mason.
        p.   cm. — (Financial sector of the American economy)
    Includes bibliographical references and index.
    ISBN 0-8153-2987-3 (alk. paper)
    1. Banks and banking—United States—History—20th
century. 2. Banking law—United States—History—20th century.
I. Title. II. Series.
HG2481.M27
332.1'2'09730904—dc21   97-40579

Printed on acid-free, 250-year-life paper
Manufactured in the United States of America

For Janice Gail White Mason,
a very loving and understanding wife.

TABLE OF CONTENTS

LIST OF TABLES

The Transformation of
Commercial Banking
in the United States,
1956–1991

CHAPTER 1
Introduction

A profound transformation of the commercial banking industry has occurred in recent years. The consolidation of local, independent banks into multi-bank holding company structures has altered the landscape of commercial banking. The scope of change is impressive (see Table 1-1). In 1956, there were approximately fourteen thousand independent commercial banks and fewer than fifty bank holding companies. By 1991, the number of independent banks had fallen to approximately three thousand, while the number of multi-bank holding companies had increased to over two thousand. In the same time period, over five thousand one-bank holding companies were formed. This book focuses on the effect of restrictive state branch banking laws on the consolidation of commercial banks in the United States. The central thesis of this study is that much of the change in the structure of commercial banking can be explained by the variation in state branch banking laws.

Change in commercial banking is occurring on three basic levels: change in the organizational form of individual commercial banks, change in state banking laws, and change in national banking laws. At the level of the individual commercial bank, the holding company form is being adopted and is displacing the traditional independent bank form. At the state level, branch banking laws are being relaxed to expand branch banking opportunities. At the federal level, restrictions on interstate branch banking have been repealed. Change in the structure of commercial banking caused by multi-bank holding company foundings and acquisitions is largely the result of state and federal restrictions on branch banking. Banks operating in

Table 1-1. Number of Commercial Banks by Type and Year

	Number of Unit Banks	Number of Multi-Bank Holding Co.	Number of One-Bank Holding Co.
1955	14479	46	117
1968	13618	106	783
1971	12063	153	1450
1980	9207	512	2393
1984	5824	1206	4896
1987	4312	1584	4919
1991	3068	2025	5463

Source: Federal Reserve Board Annual Statistical Digest.
Bank Holding Company Report, Federal Reserve Board.

states with restrictions on branch banking adopted the multi-bank holding company form as a strategy to achieve growth by evading branch banking restrictions. By forming multi-bank holding companies, banks are able to build branch banking networks through the acquisition of banks.

As recently as the early 1970s, two thirds of the states imposed some form of restriction on branch banking. One third of the states were unit banking states which meant that commercial banks were restricted to a single bank location. In other words, branch banking is strictly prohibited in unit banking states. Another one third of the states placed geographic restrictions or limits on branch banking. These states are categorized as limited branch banking states. In contrast, one third of the states placed no constraints on branch banking. These states are referred to as branch banking states. In addition to state branch banking laws, the McFadden Act of 1927 enacted federal prohibitions on branch banking by national banks unless specifically approved by state law. State and federal restrictions on branch banking in the United States served to limit competition by erecting barriers to entry in local markets which promoted the proliferation of many small, independent banks. By the mid-1990s, some type of branch banking was permitted in all fifty states, and multi-bank holding companies had diffused throughout commercial banking. In addition to changes in state branch banking laws, federal constraints on interstate branch banking were repealed in 1994.

The organization of the book is as follows. In Chapter 2, the theoretical framework used to explain the changes in the structure of commercial banking is presented. Theoretical propositions are drawn from new institutional theory in sociology and economics, organizational ecology, collective action theory, and managerial theory. In Chapter 3, I provide a brief outline of the regulatory history of commercial banking in the United States. The historical evolution of banking regulations plays an important role in shaping the direction of change that has and is continuing to occur in commercial banking. In Chapter 4, I analyze bank holding company founding and acquisition rates, as well as, bank failure rates. The results clearly demonstrate how incentives generated by state branch banking laws contributed to the observed variation in bank forms. A distinct pattern is evident in the distribution of bank forms across states according to type of branch banking law. This suggests that banks strategically adopt specific organizational forms in response to incentives imposed by state branch banking laws. In Chapter 5, a comparative analysis of bank financial performance by type of bank form and by type of state branch banking law is performed. The focus is on explaining why the bank holding company form has been successful in diffusing throughout commercial banking. The results indicate that the financial performance of multi-bank holding company subsidiaries is stronger, on average, than the financial performance of unacquired, independent banks. Bank financial performance is evaluated in terms of returns on assets and equity capital. In Chapter 6, processes related to the legitimation of the multi-bank holding company form and to changes in state branch banking laws are investigated. The discussion of the legitimation of the multi-bank holding company form and changes in state branch banking laws explores the role of selection and collective action processes in accounting for the changes that occurred. Conclusions and suggestions for future research are presented in Chapter 7.

CHAPTER 2
Theory of Change in Commercial Banking

The structure of commercial banking in the United States has experienced significant change over the past thirty years. The independent commercial bank is rapidly disappearing as bank holding companies and their subsidiaries increasingly populate the terrain of commercial banking. As recently as 1960, there were fewer than fifty bank holding companies. By 1991, over seven thousand bank holding companies had been chartered. What accounts for the change in the structure of commercial banking from 1956 to 1991?

The impetus for change in commercial banking is rooted in the economic growth era of the 1950s and 1960s (Eccles 1982). The booming post-WWII economy of the 1950s coupled with Depression era banking regulations created incentives for increased competition in the financial services industry. Financial service firms other than commercial banks began marketing innovative financial products in direct competition with the traditional services offered by commercial banks. Increasing competition within the financial services industry caused the market share of monetary assets controlled by commercial banks to shrink (see Tables 2-1 and 2-2). By the late-1950s commercial banks began to promote regulatory change to enable the use of the bank holding company form as a strategy to enhance long-term growth in lieu of increasing competition and Depression era regulatory constraints on growth and diversification opportunities. I maintain that the bank holding company form was adopted by innovative commercial banks as a growth strategy in response to restrictive state and federal banking regulations.

7

Table 2-1. Distribution of Monetary Assets Among Financial
Intermediaries 1950-1989.

| | Percentage of Total Assets | | | | |
	1950	1960	1970	1980	1990
Commercial Banks	52	38	38	36	32
Savings And Loan	6	12	14	16	12
Savings Banks	8	7	6	4	3
Credit Unions	--	1	1	2	2
Finance Companies	3	5	5	5	6
Mutual Funds	1	3	4	2	6
Money-Market Funds	--	--	--	2	5
Life Insurance Co.	22	20	15	12	13
Casualty Insurance Co.	4	5	4	5	5
Private Pension Funds	2	6	9	11	11
Public Pension Funds	2	3	5	5	7
Total %	100	100	100	100	100

Reprinted from Kaufman and Mote (1994) with permission from
the Federal Reserve Bank of Chicago.

****

Table 2-2. Composition of Short-Term Credit Market — Debt of
Non-Financial Corporate Business, 1950-1989.

	1950	1960	1970	1980	1989
		(Percentages)			
Bank Loans	91	87	83	71	60
Nonbank Finance Loans	6	9	9	14	16
Commercial Paper	1	2	6	9	12
Foreign Loans	—	—	—	1	8
Bankers' Acceptances	2	2	2	5	4
Total %	100	100	100	100	100
Dollars (billions)	20	43	125	324	903

Reprinted from Kaufman and Mote (1994) with permission from
the Federal Reserve Bank of Chicago.

In particular, three types of banking regulations have had a significant impact on commercial banking: state/federal constraints on branch banking; federal interest rate ceilings; and federal segmentation of financial markets. These constraints limited growth and diversification opportunities for commercial banks and inadvertently placed them at a competitive disadvantage with firms in the other sectors of the financial services industry. By the early 1960s, rapid advancements in computer and telecommunication technologies were beginning to reshape the terrain of the financial services industry. Technological innovations contributed to the introduction of new financial products which increased competition in the financial services industry. In addition, the "energy crisis" of the 1970s and the resultant stress on the nations' economy caused by high inflation and interest rates generated uncertainty in the banking industry. These events, combined with restrictive banking regulations, posed a threat to the survival of many commercial banks and provided the motivation for commercial banks to search for organizational strategies to evade state and federal laws constraining bank growth (Mishkin 1992:307).

Commercial banks pursuing growth through the formation of multi-bank holding companies are contributing to three types of change in commercial banking: 1) change in the dominant organizational form of individual banks: 2) change in the structure of commercial banking; and 3) change in banking laws and regulations. The first type of change, change in the organizational form of individual banks, raises the question of why banks adopt particular organizational forms. The second type of change, change in the structure of commercial banking, raises the question of how the bank holding company form diffused throughout the commercial banking industry. And the third type of change, change in banking laws, raises questions about the process leading to the legitimation of the multi-bank holding company form.

The changes in the structure of commercial banking induced by multi-bank holding companies represents the cumulative effect of individual commercial banks adapting to economic and regulatory environments. The diffusion of the multi-bank holding company form is premised on the perception of capital markets that the multi-bank holding company form through bank acquisitions can produce efficiencies which can be translated into higher returns relative to the returns generated by traditional, unitary bank forms. The proposed causal sequence of the transformation in commercial banking is: Depression era banking regulations created incentives for the founding of multi-bank holding companies; the ability of multi-bank holding companies and their bank subsidiaries to produce acceptable returns to investors; and the diffusion of the multi-bank holding company form caused changes in the structure and institutions of commercial banking. The central point of this study is that the changes in the structure and institutions of commercial banking over the observation period were caused by an interaction between banking regulations and bank growth strategies.

Hypotheses derived from institutional theory in economic sociology are formulated to explain the changes in commercial banking. The structure of commercial banking is determined by the relatively enduring practices and patterns of interaction among banks, businesses, consumers, and bank regulatory agencies. The governing institutions of commercial banking are composed of state and federal laws and regulations. These banking institutions define the incentive or payoff structure which frame the competitive strategies of commercial banks. If banks conform to the rules of the prevailing institutional framework then structural stability is expected. On the other hand, if innovative bank strategies emerge external to the prevailing framework of banking laws and regulations and the innovative practices prove successful by increasing the financial performance of banks, then it is likely that the innovative practices will be adopted by other banks and produce structural and institutional change. Change in the governing institutions of commercial banking is contingent on the legitimation of innovative banking practices. The legitimation of innovative banking practices is perceived as a function of selection processes and collective action operating at the institutional level of commercial banking.

Banking institutions in the United States consist of formal state and federal banking laws and regulations, as well as, informal norms, conventions, and political belief systems. Banking is a highly regulated industry because banks are entrusted with the prudent management of a large portion of society's monetary assets and because banking practices have a significant impact on aggregate economic activity. The fundamental rationale for government regulation of banking is to promote safe and sound banking practices to protect the interests of investors, depositors, and the general public (Huertas 1987:140; Mishkin 1992). This study focuses on the effects of a specific set of banking institutions, state branch banking laws.

State and federal restrictions on bank branch banking are contrary to the natural inclination of banks to seek expansion opportunities. Increased competition within the financial services industry in the booming post-WWII economy of the 1950s and 1960s coupled with constraints on branch banking, financial product diversification, and interest rates realigned the incentives associated with the prevailing banking regulations and increased the costs of maintaining the status quo. The changing incentive structure provided the motivation for commercial bankers to initiate a search for innovative growth strategies. The result being the adoption of the bank holding company form by commercial banks.

In summary, bank strategies are framed within the context of banking laws and regulations. Changes in bank form emerge from the interests and means of individual banks responding to the incentives generated by banking regulations set within the context of a competitive economic environment. The cumulative effect of individual bank actions circumscribe the overall structure of the commercial banking industry and its governing institutions.

Typically, organizational theories in sociology emphasize the normative effect of institutions on organizational behavior. These theories predict that organizations will adopt practices that are isomorphic with the broader institutional environment. The isomorphic effects of institutions on organizational behavior mitigates the capacity for rational and strategic action (Meyer and Rowan 1977; DiMaggio and Powell 1983). In general, organizations adopt practices that conform with institutionalized expectations in order to establish social legitimacy and acceptance. This explains the prevalence of homogeneous organizational forms within specific organizational fields. While a theory emphasizing institutional isomorphism is important in explaining conformity to institutional environments, it is does not address why an organization would pursue innovations outside the bounds of the prevailing institutional environment. By denying the feasibility of modeling interest driven, strategic behavior as an impetus for change in organizational fields, a theory premised on institutional isomorphism is incomplete and fails to adequately account for organizational or institutional dynamics.

De-emphasizing the role of strategic behavior on the part of organizations diminishes the explanatory power of a theory. Scott and Meyer (1983) acknowledge this shortcoming and attempt to reconcile the problem by conceptualizing organizations as operating in either technical or institutional environments. According to this conceptualization, technical environments are synonymous with competitive markets, and institutional environments are composed of the non-profit and public sectors of the economy. Institutional theories which emphasize organizational isomorphism and ignore strategic actions are appropriate for explaining organizational outcomes in highly institutionalized environments such as school systems, non-profit sectors, and governmental agencies. On the other hand, economic theories which stress rational behavior and neglect institutional effects are best suited for analyzing organizational outcomes in competitive, technical environments. This perspective places commercial banks in both technical and institutional environments. On the one hand, banks exist in technical environments since they are investor owned firms functioning in the highly competitive financial services industry. On the other hand, they also operate in an institutional environment since banking practices are highly regulated. Is it necessary to make the theoretical distinction between technical and institutional environments since it limits the explanatory scope of the theory (Powell 1988)?

A modified version of institutional theory from economic sociology which bridges the explanatory gap between technical and institutional environments is applied to this study of commercial banking.[1] This version of institutional theory explicitly models organizational outcomes in terms of the interaction between organizational interests and institutional constraints (Nee and Ingram 1996). Bank managers and shareholders are free to choose whether they conform or not with the prevailing banking laws and regulations.[2] Conformity is expected as long as the expected returns associated with prevailing banking laws exceed the opportunity costs of returns accruing from foregone, alternative courses of action. It is assumed that bank managers and shareholders are boundedly rational actors who attempt to realize rates of return on assets and equity comparable with similarly situated banks and desire organizational growth. Innovative banking practices which succeed in increasing investor and managerial returns are expected to diffuse as other banks attempt to imitate the relatively more successful practices. Successful innovations increase the likelihood of organizational change, and in turn, increase the likelihood of structural and institutional change within an organizational field.

Oftentimes, sociologists criticize rational actor models by pointing to the unintended, system level consequences of supposedly rational action. It is important to note that the rationality assumption of institutional theory does not imply rational social systems. The rationality of social systems cannot be deduced from the rational actions of individual units comprising the social system (North 1981, 1990). This assertion does not, in any way, undermine the primordial rationality motivating much human behavior. This is consistent with the sociological method advocated by Weber (1978:18) that

> The construction of a purely rational course of action serves the sociologists as a type which has the merit of clear understandability and lack of ambiguity. By comparison with this it is possible to understand the ways in which actual action is influenced by irrational factors of all sorts, such as effects and errors, in that they account for the deviation from the line of conduct which would be expected on the hypothesis that the action were purely rational.

By including the rationality proposition in institutional theory, it is possible to model both the normative and the dynamic effects of institutions on organizational behavior. This enables the theory to explain social processes promoting stability or change. In applying this theoretical perspective to commercial banking, bank actions can be best understood if framed within the context of incentives produced by state and federal banking regulations. To understand the underlying motives of bank actions, it is first necessary to examine the incentives produced by banking regulations bounded by the prevailing conditions of the competitive and economic environment.

Regulatory restrictions on branch banking, coupled with a shrinking market in loanable funds, set in motion a strategy of bank growth through the formation of multi-bank holding companies and bank acquisitions. Federal judicial rulings in the 1960s established that restrictions on branch banking do not apply to the subsidiaries of multi-bank holding companies (Fisher 1961; Reycraft 1972). As long as bank acquisitions do not reduce the level of competition in a local market, bank acquisitions by multi-bank holding companies are not violations of anti-trust law, and therefore, are acceptable to federal bank regulators. A bank by forming a multi-bank holding company is free to expand into desired banking markets previously denied them, and thereby, to generate a greater volume of deposits and loans to offset stagnation or saturation in the original local market. The strategy of forming multi-bank holding companies in order to acquire other banks creates a predator-prey type of relationship among individual banks. In a predator-prey environment, competitive fitness in terms of performance criteria such as returns on assets and equity plays an important role in determining the survival chances of individual banks.

Banks are motivated to generate profit levels that are satisfactory to their shareholders, as well as, to pursue growth and expansion opportunities which are likely to translate into increased compensation and prestige for bank managers. Banking profits are determined by the difference in the net income earned on loans and the costs of obtaining loanable funds. Loanable funds are generated from deposits, equity capital, and borrowed funds. Shareholders compare their returns on equity with the returns of alternative investments of comparable risk in capital markets. The inherent variability and complexity in accurately predicting the rate of returns on loanable funds, loans, and capital markets over extended periods of time makes maximizing banking returns in any absolute sense impossible. Therefore, it is assumed that bank managers are charged with the responsibility of maintaining returns on equity that are satisfactory to shareholders in a relative rather than absolute sense. Therefore, bankers are only boundedly rational with the bounds being determined by information constraints.

The efficiency of bank operations is assessed by evaluating the return on assets ratio. Return on assets is defined as the ratio of net income to total assets. Bank assets are measured by the value of their loan and investment portfolios. The level of net income produced on a given level of assets which determines variation in return on assets is a method of ascertaining the efficiency of bank management. Banks producing a high return on their assets are more able to generate profit levels satisfactory to shareholders and to finance expansion opportunities. Bank expansion into new geographic markets increases the base of loans and loanable funds with which to generate revenues. With increasing bank size in terms of its assets and liabilities, bank managers assume greater responsibilities which can be translated into greater compensation and prestige. If bank growth is managed prudently, shareholders can be expected to benefit as well. Banks desiring expansion will attempt to oppose the imposition of banking regulations that constrain growth opportunities such as restrictions on branch banking. The design of innovative practices is one method of attempting to mitigate the effects of restrictive banking regulations. The legitimacy of innovative banking practices are ultimately judged in terms of their ability to exact improvement in financial performance criteria such as returns on assets and equity.

The final element of new institutional theory is to explain how the actions of individual banks aggregate to create change in the structure and institutions of commercial banking. One approach in addressing this problem is to assume that organizational diversity is a function of selection processes. It is highly plausible to presume that financial markets select for survival those organizations that produce satisfactory returns for investors and reject those organizations that fail to produce satisfactory returns. In most instances, structural and institutional change occurs through an incremental process as managers and investors adjust to changes in the marginal returns of product markets (North 1990). The need to respond to changes at the margins produce organizational strategies that result in the genesis of innovative practices. In essence, organizational survival depends on the ability to adapt to changing environmental conditions. Organizational strategies and practices that prove successful in meeting organizational objectives spread throughout organizational fields by imitation and learning processes. A key element in organizational imitation and learning processes is the formation of associations which foster the exchange of information and ideas among member organizations. The diffusion of successful innovative practices sets in motion the process of structural change in the affected organizational field.

A formal explanation of organizational diversity premised on selection processes is organizational ecology. According to organizational ecology the founding rate of new organizational forms within a resource environment is dependent on the density of organizations competing within the resource space (Hannan and Freeman 1989; Hannan and Carroll 1991). New organizational forms such as the bank holding company are expected to diffuse slowly in the early stages of their existence when the legitimacy of the new form is low. This initial inertia is attributable to the fact that the success of the new form in meeting organization objectives has not yet been demonstrated. If a new organizational form proves effective at generating the resources required for survival over time, the legitimacy of the form increases. With increased legitimacy, the founding rate of the new form increases as others replicate it. The effects of legitimation on the founding rate of a new organizational form begins to wane with increasing density of the new form due to increasing competition for scarce resources. Eventually the founding rate of the new form begins to decrease when the carrying capacity of the resource environment is saturated. In summary, in the initial stages of a new organizational form, the founding rate of the new form increases (legitimation effect) but at a decreasing rate (competition effect). Once the carrying capacity of a resource environment is attained by the new organizational form, the founding rate of the new form begins to decline. Over the history of a particular organizational form, the founding rate is expected to be a non-monotonic function of density"first increasing then decreasing. The density dependence model of organizational founding rates is premised on the proposition that resource environments select those organizations that successfully organize resource levels adequate to meet survival needs.

Another insight of organizational ecology pertaining to the establishment of new organizational forms is the effect of prior foundings on the founding rate (Delacroix and Carroll 1983). Early adopters of a new organizational form are viewed as innovators, and if the innovative form proves successful in producing desired results, the new form is copied through imitation and learning processes. The number of recent prior foundings acts as a signal about the existence of potential profit opportunities. Therefore, an increase in the number of recent prior foundings is expected to cause an increase in the founding rate of the new organizational form. However, a very large number of recent prior foundings indicates a possible saturation of profit opportunities and leads to a decrease in the founding rate. Just as the case with density, the effect of recent prior foundings on organizational founding rates is non-monotonic. The founding rate first increases (imitation) then decreases (saturation).

Research in the organizational ecology tradition is typically over the entire history of the population of organizations being studied. However, commercial banking was a mature industry when the bank holding company form emerged as a viable growth strategy in the early 1960s. Therefore, the founding of multi-bank holding companies is an interesting case for organizational ecology. The resource environment of the multi-bank holding company form is composed of all independent commercial banks. Hence, multi-bank holding companies have a large resource pool of independent banks with which to fuel its propagation and survival. Not only are all independent banks and one-bank holding companies subject to acquisition by multi-bank holding companies, but multi-bank holding can also acquire all or part of other multi-bank holding companies. Since the multi-bank holding company movement is relatively recent in origin, the founding rate of multi-bank holding companies should be increasing over the observation period.

A weakness of the organizational ecology perspective is that it does not directly relate organizational vital rates to the enactment of formal institutions which govern organizational fields. Change in formal institutions is an exogenous influence on organizational vital rates rather than a process explained by the theory. Increasing density of an organizational form is an indicator of legitimation effects but does not explicate the institutionalization process. To address this shortcoming, a collective action model is presented to investigate the relationship between the emergence of the multi-bank holding company form and change in state branch banking laws.

As previously discussed, institutional theory explains stability and change within an organizational field in terms of the reward/cost assessments of individual organizations. The stability of the institutions that govern relations and practices within an organizational field is contingent on the degree of agreement among affected organizations that it is in their self-interest to invest in the maintenance of particular institutional arrangements (Homans 1974; Coleman 1990; Nee and Ingram 1996). The establishment and enforcement of institutional regulations within an organizational field is a function of the power relations among competing interests. An important source of institutional power is the control of scarce and valuable resources (Lenski 1966). If bankers can earn greater rewards by successfully evading branch banking regulations through the adoption of the bank holding company form and acquiring other banks in order to expand their market base, then these innovative bankers began to accumulate greater control over monetary resources relative to conforming banks. The result is a shift in the balance of power from independent bankers to multi-bank holding companies. The shift in the balance of power is likely to result in changes in banking laws and regulations which favor the interests of multi-bank holding companies.

Banks that agree to merge with bank holding companies are becoming agents of institutional change. Bankers who sell their bank to a holding company are altering the structure of the banking industry by becoming a subsidiary of a bank holding company, even if banking laws have not changed. Each additional acquisition of an independent bank by a multi-bank holding company is a step toward legitimating a new order in commercial banking. As the percentage of banks that become subsidiaries of a bank holding company increases, the balance of power shifts toward those seeking change in branch banking laws. On the other hand, it is presumed that it is in the interest of some banks to resist the encroaching hegemony of multi-bank holding companies and the erosion of constraints on branch banking by organizing opposition through the formation of banking associations.

The existence of countervailing power relations and informal institutional constraints also factor into the incremental nature of institutional change (Nee 1991; Nee and Lian 1994). The enactment of specific banking laws and regulations is determined by the relative bargaining strength of competing interests. The incentives located in laws and regulations favor the interest of some parties over the interests of others. Barriers to entry, geographical limitations on branch banking, and interest rate ceilings are examples of banking regulations which favor some set of banking interests to the detriment of other interests. If banks believe that greater returns can be realized by investing in political action to change branch banking laws, then they are expected to act on those beliefs (Mishkin 1993). It is to be expected that these changes will be opposed by other vested banking interests satisfied with the status quo and opposed to change. However, if the practices adopted by the proponents of change prove profitable and diffuse, the balance of power begins to shift in favor of the proponents of change.

Bankers act to promote and protect their interests by pursuing individual and collective strategies. Bank investors and managers must decide whether it is in their interest to pursue or resist merger and acquisition opportunities. Collective strategies are pursued by individual banks through the formation and participation in associations representing their particular interests. Banks with similar interests are expected to participate in bank associations which promote and protect their respective interests. This means that opposition within the commercial banking sector is likely to emerge between bank associations representing competing banking interests. The individual and collective strategies bankers choose reinforce either institutional stability or change.

On one side of the banking debate are independent bankers and state regulatory agencies who advocate state control of branch banking. The group representing independent bankers is the Independent Bankers Association which was formed in the 1930s to oppose bank holding companies. State bank regulatory agencies are represented by the Association of State Banking Regulatory Agencies which was founded in 1907 to oppose federal encroachment on states' rights in lieu of Congressional enactment of the Federal Reserve Act of 1913. Two associations that promoted the interests of multi-bank holding companies were the Association of Reserve City Bankers and the Association of Bank Holding Companies. These two associations merged in 1994 creating a new association named the Bankers Roundtable. In the middle of the controversy is the American Banking Association which is the peak national banking association which represents the general interests of all commercial banks.

Institutional theory proposes that institutions are nested in a hierarchy composed of lower level, informal rules which govern small group relations and of higher level, formal rules which govern organizational and societal relations (Homans 1974; North 1990; Nee and Ingram 1996). Therefore, the course of institutional change is greatly influenced by the interaction of formal and informal institutions, and the process is dependent on past history. The costs of attempting to change higher level institutions such as national banking laws is greater than attempts to change lower level institutions such as state banking laws. Attempts to change higher level institutions are often stymied or compromised by the stickiness of informal institutions such as norms, conventions, and ideologies arising from social and economic networks. Two informal factors which are important to owners and managers of independent banks are the power and prestige they have in their communities. These informal instutional arrangements oftentimes impede the ability of multi-bank holding companies to acquire independent banks. Before state and federal branch banking laws are changed, some type of consensus must first emerge among independent bankers that the multi-bank holding company form presents options to their long-term interests. Opposition to multi-bank holding companies decreases as they increase in number and build political alliances. Through interest group mobilization, the legitimation process initiated at the local level is translated into pressure on state and federal authorities to repeal branch banking restrictions. Hence, changes in state branch banking laws are expected to precede changes in federal branch banking laws.

Coexisting with sociological theories of organizations are various economic theories of organizations. Traditional economic theories of organizations assume that managers are rational agents who attempt to maximize profits through activities designed to promote organizational efficiency. Economic theory would explain the adoption of the bank holding company strategy and the ensuing changes in the structure of commercial banking strictly in terms of competitive market forces and largely ignore the effects of institutions external to the firm. One of the primary reasons commercial bankers form bank holding companies and acquire banks is to realize scale and scope economies, thereby reducing unit costs and increasing profitability. Scale economies are achieved by increasing the utilization of bank resources and technologies by increasing the overall volume of business. Scope economies are attained from synergies achieved through the utilization of a core staff and facilities in reducing the amount of duplication in services provided throughout the expanding bank network. However study after study examining scale and scope economies in commercial banking conclude that banks realize minimum marginal costs at a relatively modest size, somewhere in the $100 to $200 million range of assets (Rose 1988:82; Humphrey 1990: Boyd and Graham 1993:138). This body of research challenges the economic hypotheses premised on the efficiencies of scale and scope economies since much of the restructuring of commercial banking is being caused by bank holding companies with assets greater than $200 million. Another interesting finding of these studies suggests that diseconomies of scale are realized as banks grow very large, somewhere in the two billion dollar asset range.

Another important variant of economic theory is transaction cost analysis. One of the focuses of the transaction cost approach to organizational research is on explaining the evolution of organizational forms. The historical development of the firm has evolved from small, owner controlled businesses, to cartels, to holding companies, to unitary corporations, and to the multi-divisional form. The transaction cost theory of the firm is based on the idea that organizational structures are designed in an attempt to reduce transaction costs attributed to opportunism and bounded rationality (Williamson 1975:144, 1985:281). This body of research calls into question the efficacy of the holding company organizational form. A holding company is defined a loosely coupled management structure where each of the firms controlled by the holding company retain a semi-autonomous identity. Since the units comprising a holding company are semi-autonomous, there are inherent structural constraints on the internal flow of information which inhibits the integration, control, and coordination of internal functions. A further weakness of the holding company form derives from higher transaction costs linked with the gathering and processing of information, as well as, with the monitoring and enforcement of performance standards within and between its semi-autonomous units. Hence, the holding company form exacerbates rather than reduces the costs of opportunism and bounded rationality. If the holding company form is less efficient than an integrated organizational form, then what explains the recent proliferation of the multi-bank holding company form?

A prominent organizational theory addressing mergers and acquisitions in American industry is managerial theory. Managerial theory postulates that managers of modern corporations are maximizers of growth and organization size rather than profits and shareholder returns (Marris 1964; Mueller 1986). Managerial salaries and prestige are more closely related to organizational growth and size than with profitability. Due to incentive structures, managers are more likely than owners to pursue growth strategies. The managerial perspective explains the popularity of acquisitions and mergers by conglomerates controlled by managers which cannot be explained by increased efficiency or improved financial performance arguments. The assertion that growth strategies dominate profit criteria has been challenged in recent years by the large number of conglomerate divestments (Davis, Diekmann, and Tinsley 1994). Since the bank holding company movement begins during the peak conglomerate merger and acquisition wave of the 1960s and reaches its peak during the divestment wave of the 1980s, the relationship of efficiency and profitability of bank holding companies will be closely examined in this study. Therefore, it is reasonable to assume that while managers and owners value growth, it is unreasonable to assume that they can deviate very far from profit maximization without being disciplined by the market (Caves 1982).

Economic theories with their strict emphasis on the internal characteristics of individual firms fail to fully take into account the oftentimes substantial effects of industry level institutions on organizational behavior at the level of the firm. I argue that the adoption of the bank holding company form is the result of an interaction effect between banking institutions and the interests of individual banks. If field level institutions are not a causal factor in the formation of bank holding companies then what accounts for the systematic variation in bank forms across state branch banking regimes?

This completes the general theoretical outline which informs this study of bank holding companies and the transformation of commercial of banking in the United States from 1956 through 1991. In Chapters 4 through 6, I apply the various theoretical propositions presented in this chapter to explain the structural and institutional transformation of commercial banking. In each of the following chapters, I elaborate on the general propositions presented in this chapter and derive hypotheses which are formally tested with the statistical analyses of bank data. But first, before I present the formal bank analyses, I present a brief historical sketch of banking regulations in the United States.

NOTES

1. This representation of institutional theory is the author's interpretation of a series of new institutional theory seminars conducted by Victor Nee at Cornell University between 1992 and 1994. For a more complete presentation of the theory see Nee and Ingram (1996). Competing versions of institutional theory are currently popular in both economics and sociology. The version of institutional theory I present is an explicit attempt to reconcile differences pertaining to the underlying behavioral assumptions between the two disciplines.

2. Note that I am defining individual banks as individual corporate actors which is a conceptually distinct level from individual human actors. I assume that the same behavioral assumptions which govern individual human actors can be applied to corporate actors.

CHAPTER 3

The Regulatory History of Commercial Banking

To comprehend the direction of change in social structures it is important to understand the history leading to present conditions. In other words, history matters. As previously stated, the bank holding company movement raises interesting questions since organizational researchers routinely dismiss the holding company form as a relatively inefficient artifact of the late nineteenth and early twentieth centuries (Chandler 1962; Williamson 1985). A history of organizational forms in the United States is commonly viewed as a progression from single owners to cartels to holding companies to unitary forms to multi-divisional forms (Chandler 1962, 1977; Williamson 1975, 1985; Fligstein 1985, 1990, 1991). In light of this body of research, the organizational form of commercial banking is lagging far behind the general trend. In attempting to understand the structure of commercial banking it is important to recognize the role of the state. The state through its regulatory and enforcement powers is perceived as a powerful actor in determining the trajectory of forms which organizations adopt (Meyer and Rowan 1977; DiMaggio and Powell 1983; Fligstein 1996). This is particularly the case with the historical development of banking forms in the United States and the current trend toward the bank holding company form.

From the nation's founding, states have assumed the authority to charter and regulate banks operating within their borders. The legitimation of states' banking powers is embedded within the political ideology of states' rights. States' rights is premised on the notion that economic and political power is to be decentralized. The structure of the banking industry has been heavily influenced by this ideology since the nation's founding (Hammond 1957).

The First Bank of the United States (1792-1812) and the Second Bank of the United States (1816-1836) were two aborted attempts at establishing a centrally controlled, national banking system. Opposition to a centralized, national banking system was led by states' rights advocates who proclaimed the merits of state control of banking. Andrew Jackson became the champion of decentralized banking, and state control of banking became firmly rooted during the Jacksonian era of the 1830s.

Under the Jackson administration, widespread agrarian opposition to banks in general and to a national central bank in particular led to the collapse of the Second Bank of the United States and ushered in a period of "free banking" (Hammond 1957). The states' rights argument was premised on the idea that small local banks would better serve the financial needs of local communities than would large national banks. Also, states claimed that they would be more likely to promote the viability of relatively small, local banks from the threat of competitive encroachment by large urban and national banks. State legislatures and state banking agencies protect small local banks by controlling competition and bank expansion through charter powers and branch banking regulations.

The legal codification of states' rights in banking regulation inadvertently occurred with Congressional passage of the National Bank Act of 1863. The National Bank Act of 1863 was the nation's first comprehensive effort to establish a national banking system and a unified monetary system. Through interpretation of the National Bank Act of 1863, national banks were restricted to "one brick and mortar office." Although this phrase was not actually included in the language of the Act itself, subsequent amendments to the Act reinforced this interpretation. Since the enactment of the National Bank Act of 1863, the federal government has consistently delegated to the states the authority to regulate intra- and inter-state branch banking. The resulting state regulations created three types of state banking regimes: unit banking states, limited branch banking states, and branch banking states. Unit banking states strictly prohibit branch banking, thereby, limiting a bank's operations to one location. Limited branch banking states place geographic limits on the distance a branch bank may be located from the main office such as a specific city, county, contiguous counties, or other regional variations. Branch banking states allow banks to establish branch banks throughout the state. State restrictions on branch banking generated a banking industry populated by thousands of small, local banks. By 1900 there were over 20,000 commercial banks operating in the United States. By the 1920s this number had swelled to over 30,000 commercial banks.

State authority to limit branch banking was subsequently upheld by the Federal Reserve Act of 1913, the McFadden Act of 1927, and the National Bank Acts of 1933 and 1935. The McFadden Act of 1927 vested the power to regulate intra-state branch banking by national banks with the individual states and explicitly prohibited inter-state branch banking by national banks. The Depression era banking reforms (National Bank Acts of 1933 and 1935) were designed to promote safe and sound banking practices by limiting competition among banks (Friedman and Schwartz 1963:443-44; Mishkin 1992:59-60). To accomplish this end, the Banking Acts of 1933 and 1935 segmented financial markets along product lines, regulated interest rates on deposits, and maintained geographical restrictions on bank expansion (see Table 3-1).

A significant component of the Bank Acts of 1933 (sections 16, 20, 21, and 32 collectively known as the Glass-Steagall Act) was the separation of banking and security businesses. Also, the National Bank Act of 1933 prohibited payment of interest on demand deposits (checking accounts) which was a banking service that only commercial banks could offer. The National Banking Act of 1935 created Regulation Q interest rate ceilings on time deposits at all federally insured banks. The maximum rate of interest on deposits for commercial were set lower than the maximum rate allowed savings and loan banks. The differential in interest rates provided a competitive advantage to savings and loans banks in attracting time deposits. This advantage was provided to savings and loan banks in order to promote home ownership in the United States (Mishkin 1992:61). Savings and loan banks were authorized to make only mortgage loans, not commercial or consumer loans. The rationale for interest rate ceilings on deposits was the widespread belief at the time that unrestricted interest rate competition contributed to the severity of the Great Depression.

In return for agreement to the segmentation of financial services, commercial banks were granted a monopoly on the right to both receive demand deposits and make commercial loans. These banking regulations provided incentives for bankers in the form of limited competition and insulated product markets. Commercial banking as a distinct entity within the broader framework of the financial services industry is strictly a political

Table 3-1. Federal Banking Laws — Chronological Listing

Charter for First Bank of the United States (1791-1811)
— Congress granted a 20 year charter in 1791 and refused to renew the charter in 1811.
Charter for Second Bank of the United States (1816-1836)
— Congress granted a 20 year charter in 1816 and refused to renew the charter in 1836.
Free Banking Era (1837-1862)
— in 1837 Michigan became first state to pass a free banking law whereby anyone could open a bank by meeting minimum capital requirements
— by 1860 eighteen of the then thirty-two states had passed free banking statutes
National Bank Act of 1863
— authorized branches of national banks only for previously owned branches of state banks converting to national banks
Federal Reserve Act (1913)
— required all national banks to become members of Federal Reserve system and provided an option for eligible state banks to join
McFadden Act (1927)
— permitted national banks (with approval of Office of Comptroller of the Currency) and state member banks (with approval of the Federal Reserve Board) to branch in their home cities to the extent that state banks were similarly permitted by state law; as a result, national banks were not permitted to branch across state lines
Banking Act of 1933 (sections 16, 20, 21, and 32 known as the Glass-Steagall Act)
— prohibited payment of interest on demand deposits
— gave the Federal Reserve Board authority to impose interest rate ceilings on time and savings deposits at member banks
— created the Federal Deposit Insurance Corporation and provided for deposit insurance
— sec. 16 prohibited national banks and state member banks from purchasing equities and prohibited their underwriting and dealing in securities other than U.S. Treasury securities, agency obligations, and general state and municipal obligations
— sec. 20 prohibited member banks from affiliating with organizations engaged principally in securities activities

Table 3-1, *continued.*

- sec. 21 prohibited a person engaged in securities business from receiving deposits (with some exceptions for state-chartered banks)
- sec. 32 prohibited interlocking directorates between member banks and securities firms unless authorized by the Federal Reserve Board

Banking Act of 1935

- gave the Federal Reserve Board the authority to adjust reserve requirements within specified ranges
- authorized ceilings on interest rates on time and savings deposits at all federally insured banks

Bank Holding Company Act of 1956

- gave the Federal Reserve Board the primary responsibility for supervising and regulating multi-bank holding companies, in order to avoid restraint of trade in banking and to maintain a separation between commerce and banking by permitting holding companies to engage only in nonbanking activities that are closely related to banking
- provided that a bank holding company operating in one state may not acquire a bank in a second state unless that state expressly authorizes the acquisition by statute
- grandfathered existing interstate bank holding companies to place certain nonbank affiliates in other states

Bank Merger Acts of 1960 and 1966

- prohibited mergers between an insured bank and a noninsured institution without approval of the Federal Deposit Insurance Corporation
- prohibited mergers of any two insured banks without approval of (1) the Office of the Comptroller of the Currency if the resulting bank is to be a national bank, (2) the Federal Reserve Board if the resulting bank is to be a state member bank, or (3) the Federal Deposit Insurance Corporation if the resulting bank is to be a nonmember insured bank
- specified that mergers were not to be approved if they would create a monopoly or if they would substantially lessen competition unless anti-competitive effects were clearly outweighed by convenience and needs of the community
- authorized the Justice Department to bring suit under anti-trust laws to prevent a proposed merger

Table 3-1, *continued*

1966 Amendments to the Bank Holding Company Act
— made the factors that the Federal Reserve Board is to consider in acting on bank holding company applications conform to those designated in the 1966 Bank Merger Act
— defined a bank as an institution accepting demand deposits

1970 Amendments to the Bank Holding Company Act
— extended the Federal Reserve Board's authority over bank holding companies to one-bank holding companies
— broadened somewhat the exceptions to the prohibition against bank holding companies engaging in nonbanking activities

1970 Amendments to the Bank Holding Company Act (continued)
— defined a bank as an institution accepting demand deposits and making commercial loans

Depository Institutions Deregulation and Monetary Control Act of 1980
— provided a six-year phase-out of Regulation Q ceilings on time and savings deposit interest rates
— eliminated Federal Reserve requirements on personal time and savings deposits
— required Federal Reserve Board to provide nonmember banks and thrift institutions such services as borrowing at discount window, check clearing, safekeeping of securities, wire transfers, automatic clearinghouse facilities, and cash transportation services
— authorized savings and loan associations to invest up to 20 percent of assets in consumer loans, commercial paper, and corporate debt securities; to issue credit cards; and to exercise trust powers
— authorized mutual savings banks to make commercial, corporate, and business loans up to 5 percent of assets

Garn-St Germain Depository Institutions Act of 1982
— authorized thrift institutions to invest in state government securities; to make commercial and agriculture loans up to 10 percent of assets; and to accept deposits from businesses with which a loan relationship had been established
— authorized various actions by regulatory agencies to assist troubled institutions, including approval of emergency acquisitions across state lines

construction. The initial response of the banking industry to the Depression era reforms was positive since they provided a welcomed breathing space in which to recover from the cataclysmic events of the Depression years.

The Bank Acts of 1933 and 1935 virtually ignored the issue of bank holding companies. While group and chain banking had been very popular in the 1920s, the effects of the Depression caused the breakup of all but a few of the group and chain banks. A serious obstacle to the formation of bank holding companies was a hostile political environment to holding companies in general. In 1930, legislation was sponsored in Congress opposing bank holding companies and similar legislation was introduced in every Congress from 1935 through 1955 (Fisher 1961; Rose 1986). While legislation against holding companies was not enacted, the political environment of the 1930s and 1940s created considerable uncertainty about the future of bank holding companies and served as a significant constraint on the adoption of the holding company form (Fisher 1961:75). From 1933 through 1956 there were fewer than 50 multi-bank holding companies in the United States. The primary opposition to bank holding companies was organized by the Independent Bankers Association which was founded in the early 1930s, and whose membership base is composed primarily of town and country banks often referred to as "Main Street" banks.

A particularly salient obstacle to bank mergers and acquisitions in the 1950s was uncertainty regarding anti-trust law. If a bank holding company buys a bank in a given locality, it is susceptible to antitrust action if the acquisition significantly reduces competition in the acquired bank's service area. The judicial definition of antitrust is based on Section 7 of the Clayton Act which defines competition in terms of market share. Even though regulation of bank-holding company mergers and acquisitions is the jurisdiction of the Board of Governors of the Federal Reserve, there exists the threat that the Justice Department will acquiesce to political pressure and initiate antitrust litigation independent of the Board of Governors of the Federal Reserve. The perceived threat and costs of antitrust litigation in the 1950s raised uncertainty and constituted a significant constraint on bank growth through acquisitions and mergers.

Until the 1950s, judicial interpretations of the Sherman Anti-Trust Act and the Clayton Act had precluded banks. If anti-trust action was to be initiated in banking it was the believed to be the responsibility of the Board of Governors of the Federal Reserve System. The first anti-trust case brought against a bank by the Federal Reserve Board was against the multi-state banking empire of Transamerica Corporation (Fisher 1961; Reycraft 1972). The Federal Reserve Board lost its case on Transamerica's appeal before the Supreme Court in 1953. The United States Congress intervened in the Transamerica case and forced the break-up of Transamerica Corporation through Congressional legislation. This unusual case clearly demonstrated the need for legislation to demarcate the legal boundaries of the bank holding company. The initial Congressional effort coming in the form of the Bank Holding Company Act of 1956.

Ironically, the Bank Holding Company Act of 1956 represented a victory of sorts for the proponents of bank holding companies because the Act provided the first legal definition of a multi-bank holding company. Also of major significance, the Act did not contain language hostile to the formation of bank holding companies. A bank holding company was defined as any company which directly or indirectly owns, controls, or holds power to vote 25 percent or more of the voting shares of two or more banks. The Bank Holding Company Act of 1956 prohibited bank holding companies from owning more than 5 percent of the voting shares of any company engaged in non-banking activities and limited them to the operation of only those non-bank firms that provided products closely related to banking. One-bank holding companies were not included in the Act because it was believed that the only way to get the legislation passed was to exempt one-bank holding companies from the legislation. The key obstacle to including one- bank holding companies was the 5 percent ownership of non-banking firms (Fisher 1961). Hence, a one-bank holding company remained a viable alternative for bank diversification. The Bank Holding Company Act was amended in 1970 to include one-bank holding companies.

The Bank Holding Company Act of 1956 stated that a bank holding company operating in one state may not acquire a bank in another state unless that state expressly authorized the acquisition by statute. The Federal Reserve Board was given the primary responsibility for supervising and regulating multi-bank holding companies. While submitting bank holding companies to the regulatory powers of the Federal Reserve Board and limiting their subsidiaries to activities closely related to banking, the Bank Holding Company Act of 1956 became the basis for court interpretations of multi-bank holding company acquisitions which set the stage for the subsequent restructuring of banking in the United States. However, the multi-bank holding company was not yet an attractive growth alternative. Uncertainty still existed regarding the legal and regulatory boundaries of the Bank Holding Company Act of 1956 due to a lack of court rulings on bank mergers and acquisitions.

In 1960 Congress passed the Bank Merger Act of 1960 which authorized the Federal Reserve Board to bring suit against anti-competitive bank mergers and acquisitions. The wording of the Bank Merger Act of 1960 was ambiguous and was a cause of concern to the Justice Department. Because of dissatisfaction with the Bank Merger Act of 1960, The Justice Department began to closely review all bank mergers and acquisitions (Johnson and Johnson 1985:492). The first successful Justice Department antitrust case in commercial banking occurred in 1963 when the Justice Department brought antitrust action against Philadelphia National Bank who was attempting to acquire another Philadelphia bank (Reycraft 1972:32; Hawawini and Swary 1990:9). Bank mergers were thought to be exempt from anti-trust action under the Sherman and Clayton Antitrust Acts. However, the Supreme Court in the Philadelphia National Bank case ruled that Section 7 of the Clayton Act—that no merger or acquisition be approved if it substantially lessens competition—applied to bank mergers and acquisitions. The Philadelphia National Bank case set a precedent for the potential involvement of the Justice Department in bank mergers and acquisitions. The Justice Department continued to be involved in the litigation of anti-trust cases involving bank mergers and acquisitions in the early 1960s and provided an additional barrier to the use of the multi-bank holding company as a means of entry into new markets for banks (Hawawini and Swary 1990).

In an attempt to untangle the regulatory maze confronting bank mergers and acquisitions, Congress enacted the Bank Merger Act of 1966 (80 Stat. 7, 12 U.S.C. 1828) which explicitly specifies the appropriate regulatory agencies for bank mergers and acquisitions involving different classifications of commercial banks (e.g. acquisitions by Federal Reserve member banks versus acquisitions by non-Federal Reserve member banks). Most importantly, the 1966 Bank Merger Act set a thirty day deadline for Justice Department antitrust challenges to bank mergers and acquisitions from the date that the merger or acquisition application is finalized by the Federal Reserve Board. In addition, the Justice Department in 1968 published general merger and acquisition guidelines. The sum effect of the antitrust court cases and the subsequent merger guidelines was to substantially reduce uncertainty and potential litigation costs associated with bank mergers and acquisitions. The clarification of legal issues proved a stimulant for multi-bank holding company activity. The codification of court tested bank merger and acquisition guidelines contained in the Bank Merger Act of 1966 and the publication of Justice Department guidelines were followed by a significant increase in the number multi-bank holding company foundings and acquisitions. Organizational researchers have focused much attention on the corporate merger wave that occurred in the 1960s. It appears that the bank merger wave of the 1960s lags behind the non-banking corporate merger wave due to the uncertainty regarding the regulatory jurisdiction of bank mergers and acquisitions.

The anti-trust laws were designed to protect competitive business environments. Section 7 of Clayton Act states that the purpose of anti-trust law is to prevent anti-competitive practices in any part of the country which leaves a lot of room to maneuver in determining the boundaries of competitive markets. Three key criteria in ruling on the appropriateness of bank mergers are population of market, bank concentration within the local market set in the context of the number of banks in a state, and the potential level of competition in a market arising from de novo entry (Reycraft 1972:125-51). Hence, the courts' interpretation of market share becomes a critical issue. Because of barriers to entry in banking markets created by prohibitive branch banking laws, local banking markets are generally concentrated in the hands of four to seven banks. If courts interpret market share in terms of local banking markets, then bank acquisitions represent a large percentage increase in market share which increases the likelihood of a merger being ruled anti-competitive. On the other hand, if market share is interpreted as the entire state, then each acquisition represents a much smaller percentage of the total market. Research has indicated that court interpretations of market share in bank merger and acquisition decisions in the 1960s hinged primarily on the number of banks in a state.

In markets with small populations, market share does not seem to be very important in court merger decisions. However, once a relatively modest threshold of population density is attained concentration of market share becomes prominent. In general, research findings suggest that when four or fewer banks control a high percentage of the market then an acquisition of one of these banks in that market is unlikely to meet approval even when the acquisition represents a very small percentage of the market (Reycraft 1972:125-51). Therefore, large banks in concentrated markets generally must look to other geographic markets for expansion opportunities through bank acquisition. Also, the courts have based bank merger and acquisition rulings on subjective criteria such as whether or not a bank *would* be likely to expand de novo into a particular market, and thereby, increase competition. If it can be shown that a bank has the motivation to expand into a particular market de novo then entry through acquisition is more likely to be denied by the courts.

In summary, Congressional banking legislation and judicial rulings in the 1950-1966 period cleared the way for the bank holding company form to be used as a strategy to evade state branch banking restrictions. In the 1956-1965 period there were 31 multi-bank holding company foundings and 477 bank acquisitions. In the five year period following passage of the Bank Merger Act of 1966 there were 111 multi-bank holding company foundings and 412 bank acquisitions. These numbers clearly suggest that clarification in laws and regulations governing multi-bank holding companies enabled bankers to adopt the multi-bank holding company form as a viable growth strategy.

CHAPTER 4

Structural Change in Commercial Banking, 1956-1991

The structure of commercial banking in the United States is defined by the relatively enduring patterns of banking practices and is governed by state and federal banking laws. Incremental changes in the structure of commercial banking is expected as bankers respond to the natural evolution of technological and market environments and is not of particular theoretical interest. However, commercial banking is experiencing extensive and rapid change in its structure and governing institutions which does call for explanation. In 1956, commercial banks were overwhelmingly composed of unitary, independent banks. The structure of commercial banking is being transformed through the formation of one-bank and multi-bank holding companies. The United States has a long history of promoting local, independent banks, and the extensive consolidation of local, independent banks into state-wide, regional, and national banks represents a radical change in the structure of commercial banking. Banks are increasingly forced to choose between forming a one-bank holding company, forming a multi-bank holding company, being acquired by a multi-bank holding company, or remaining independent. I maintain that the type of organizational form banks choose varies according to the competitive conditions imposed on banks by the content of specific types of state branch banking laws. In this chapter, I investigate the effects of state branch banking laws on the decisions of banks to adopt particular bank forms.

Federal and state banking regulations define the boundaries of legitimate banking practices and limit bank options to pursue profit and growth opportunities. I assume that bank managers strive to devise competitive strategies to produce desired profit and growth levels. Bank preferences and strategies are conditioned by both banking regulations and the capital resources of the bank. Branch banking regulations are important influences on bank behavior for they define the geographic boundaries of banking markets. Banks, as do other businesses, weigh their expected returns from one course of action against the foregone returns from alternative business opportunities. If expected returns to be realized from compliance with prevailing banking regulations are sufficient to insure bank survival then compliance is expected. However, if the expected returns do not insure bank survival and if potentially profitable opportunities exist outside the range of banking practices defined by regulatory, it is to be expected that banks will search for innovative practices to realize the gains from denied opportunities.

Banking regulations having the greatest impact on the structure of banking incentives are; the segmentation of financial markets granted commercial banks a monopoly on interest free demand deposits (checking accounts) but prohibited from engaging in investment banking; interest rate differentials on demand and time deposits—commercial banks prohibited commercial banks from offering interest on demand deposits in return for a lower maximum rate that they could offer on time deposits in relation to savings and loan banks; state and federal restrictions on inter- and intra-state branch banking; and federal deposit insurance providing limited protection to bank depositors. The intent of these regulations was to reduce the number of bank failures in order to maintain a safe and sound banking system (Kaufman 1992; Mishkin 1992). To accomplish this end, bank regulations were designed to limit competition and to stabilize profits within financial markets. The creation of insulated markets and stable profit margins were positive incentives built into the regulations to gain the approval of bankers. In the 1930s and 1940s, the regulations were acceptable to commercial bankers since growth opportunities for commercial banks were virtually nonexistent due to a depressed economy, and the high risk of bank failure was still a recent memory. Economic stagnation causing a low demand for business loans created a surplus supply of bank reserves and loanable funds which precluded bank expansion. With the return of economic prosperity in the post-WWII boom years, the demand for loans increased dramatically as businesses sought financing to expand their production capabilities to meet long arrested consumer demand. By the end of the 1940s, the surplus of loanable funds had disappeared, and capital demand exceeded supply (Fisher

1961; Eccles 1982). With the growth economy of the 1950s and 1960s, some banks began to perceive a tightening in the loanable funds market due to increased demand for loans and to increasing competition in the capital funds market. These conditions altered the effects of Depression era regulations; the costs of restrictive regulations began to outweigh the benefits accruing from protected markets for some banks (Eisenbeis 1987:21). However, most commercial banks through the 1960s were quite satisfied with the prevailing state and federal banking regulations since they maintained stable markets and provided an inexpensive source of loanable funds (Burns 1988:6-7).

As robust economic growth persisted through the 1960s, the market rate of interest on capital reserves continued to exceed the regulated rate offered by commercial banks. Expanding businesses with large cash reserves began to increasingly invest in the commercial paper market in order to realize market interest rates on their cash reserves. Not only were banks losing corporate deposits to money market financial instruments, individuals were increasingly transferring their commercial bank deposits to savings and loan banks to take advantage of the higher interest rates as a hedge against increasing inflation rates. The net effect of interest rate regulations on commercial banking was a decreasing share in the market for monetary assets from 1950-1970 (see Tables 2-1 and 2-2). The long-term implications of shrinking deposit and loan markets due to increased competition within the financial services industry began to be growing concern to commercial bankers. In response, commercial bankers began a search for growth strategies to circumvent regulatory constraints (Eccles 1982:115-16; Koch 1992:67; Mishkin 1992:307).

Commercial bankers could achieve growth through expansion of services into new market areas and/or by providing a more diversified range of financial products, but they were prohibited from pursuing these options because of banking regulations. Therefore, commercial bankers began to explore the feasibility of the holding company form to legally circumvent banking regulations. By the mid-1960s court rulings, bank merger legislation, and Department of Justice merger guidelines began to clarify the legal issues surrounding bank acquisitions by bank holding companies. With passage of the Bank Merger Act of 1966 (80 Stat. 7, PL 356) and the Justice Department's (1968) merger and acquisition guidelines, it became increasingly evident to commercial banks that they had the option of choosing among four organizational forms to pursue long-term growth and diversification objectives: 1) to remain an independent bank; 2) to form a multi-bank holding company and acquire other commercial banks; 3) to be acquired by a multi-bank holding company; and 4) to form a one-bank holding company. The calculus of payoffs/costs associated with these different growth strategies are determined to a great extent by the content of state branch banking laws in the states where banks operate.

Since the enactment of the National Bank Act of 1863, the federal government has delegated to the individual states' the authority to regulate branch banking, and in response, states have implemented a variety of branch banking laws. Based on type of branch banking law, states are categorized as unit banking states, limited branch banking states, and branch banking states. Unit banking states strictly prohibit branch banking, thereby, limiting a bank to one "brick and mortar" location. In 1956, there were seventeen unit bank states (see Table 4-1). Limited branch banking states place a limit on the distance a branch may be located from the main office such as city, county, contiguous counties, or other regional variations. In 1956, there were fifteen limited branch banking states. The number of limited branch banking states has increased due to unit bank states liberalizing their branch banking laws. Branch banking states allow banks to establish branches statewide. In 1956, there were nineteen branch banking states.

The dynamics driving the formation of multi-bank holding companies is believed to be different from those driving the formation of one-bank holding companies. The formation of multi-bank holding companies is a strategy best suited for market expansion in lieu of branch banking restrictions. Whereas, the formation of one-bank holding companies is a strategy designed to achieve either product diversification or to defend against acquisition (Cooper and Fraser 1984; Johnson and Johnson 1985; Koch 1988; Austin 1989). All commercial banks are equally affected by federal laws segmenting financial markets, but only commercial banks in unit banking states are completely denied expansion opportunities through branch banking. Hence, it is reasonable to assume that banks in unit banking states would be the most interested in formation of multi-bank holding companies to expand into new geographic markets through bank acquisition. On the other hand, banks in states that allow branch or limited branch banking are able to expand their markets through branch banking and are

Table 4-1. State Banking Laws — Branch and Interstate Banking

| | Branch Banking Laws | | | | Interstate | |
	1961	1976	1983	1989	Type*	Enacted
Alabama	L	L	L	B	R	'87
Alaska	B	B	B	B	N	'82
Arizona	B	B	B	B	N	'86
Arkansas	U	U	L	B	R	'89
California	B	B	B	B	R/T	'87
Colorado	U	U	U	U	R/T	'88
Connecticut	B	B	B	B	R	'83
Delaware	B	B	B	B	R/T	'88
Florida	U	U	L	L	R	'85
Georgia	L	L	L	L	R	'85
Hawaii	B	B	B	B	—	—
Idaho	B	B	B	B	N	'88
Illinois	U	U	U	L	R/T	'86
Indiana	L	L	L	L	R/T	'87
Iowa	U	U	L	L	—	—
Kansas	U	U	U	L	N	'47
Kentucky	L	L	L	L	N	'86
Louisiana	L	L	L	L	R/T	'87
Maine	B	B	B	B	N	'78
Maryland	B	B	B	B	R	'85
Massachusetts	L	L	L	B	R	'83
Michigan	L	L	L	L	R/T	'86
Minnesota	U	U	L	L	R	'86
Mississippi	L	L	L	L	R	'88
Missouri	U	U	U	L	R	'86
Montana	U	U	U	U	—	—
Nebraska	U	U	U	L	R/T	'90
Nevada	B	B	B	B	R/T	'85
New Hampshire	U	L	B	B	R	'87
New Jersey	L	L	B	B	N	'88
New Mexico	L	L	L	L	N	'90
New York	L	L	B	B	N	'82
North Carolina	B	B	B	B	R	'85
North Dakota	U	U	U	U	—	—
Ohio	L	L	L	B	R/T	'85
Oklahoma	U	U	U	L	N	'87
Oregon	B	B	B	B	R/T	'86
Pennsylvania	L	L	L	L	R/T	'86
Rhode Island	B	B	B	B	N	'88
South Carolina	B	B	B	B	R	'86
South Dakota	B	B	B	B	N	'88
Tennessee	L	L	L	B	R	'85
Texas	U	U	U	L	N	'87
Utah	B	B	B	B	N	'88
Vermont	B	B	B	B	R/T	'88
Virginia	L	B	B	B	R	'85
Washington	B	B	B	B	N	'87
West Virginia	U	U	U	B	N	'88
Wisconsin	U	L	L	L	R	'87
Wyoming	U	U	U	U	N	'87

U = Unit State   L = Limited Branch State   B = Branch State
*N = Nationwide   *R = Regional Reciprocity Required
*R/T = Regional Reciprocity Required/Trigger to Nationwide

more likely to be interested in extending their range of financial products and services through the formation of one-bank holding companies.

There are several valid reasons for banks to desire expansion. For one, restrictions on branch banking is an impediment to increasing the deposit and loan base of commercial banks. Also, geographic restrictions prevent commercial banks from being able to diversify the risks associated with being constrained to the economic fortunes of local markets. A bank can expand into desired markets in two ways. It can found branches de novo in states that allow branch banking, or it can acquire an existing bank which is particularly relevant in unit banking states. Often, it is cheaper and less risky for a bank to expand geographically through the acquisition of existing banks. This is true for two reasons: first, expansion by acquisition instantaneously produces an established customer base and the associated accumulated customer goodwill; and second, the acquisition of established banks minimizes the risk of failure due to a liability of newness (Rose 1988). The primary motivations for acquiring banks are to increase the supply of loanable funds and borrowers, to increase market share and power, and to hedge risk.

The multi-bank holding company form is able to evade state restrictions on branch banking because each bank held by the holding company is autonomous with respect to the other bank subsidiaries. In this manner, unit banks are able to form a holding company and expand into desired banking markets previously denied them. The only obstacle to the use of the holding company form as a growth vehicle are federal anti-trust laws which seek to prevent acquisitions that significantly decrease the level of competition in banking markets. Anti-trust litigation can be avoided through the acquisition of banks located in market areas other than their own since Supreme Court interpretations of banking concentration is determined by local market share (Johnson and Johnson 1985:493).

Since commercial banks in branch and limited branch banking states are able to achieve growth through branch banking, the one-bank holding company form in branch and limited branch states is a means of realizing financial product diversification. The Bank Holding Company Act of 1956 allows subsidiaries of bank holding companies to engage in services that are "closely related to banking." A one-bank holding company is able to offer products and services such as data processing and bookkeeping services, some types of investment brokerage and insurance underwriting, credit card companies, mortgage banking, etc. which are tailored to specific markets in their service area (Johnson and Johnson 1985:497). A one-bank holding company can either charter de novo or acquire firms to market a variety financial products. The one-bank holding company form does not violate the principles of segmented financial markets since the non-bank subsidiaries are autonomous legal entities with respect to the lead commercial bank of the one-bank holding company structure. The one-bank holding company form can also be used as a defensive strategy to prevent a hostile takeover by insulating the lead bank and increasing buyout costs. This is a viable strategy for banks wanting to remain independent (Austin 1989). This would be a particularly salient option for independent banks in branch and limited branch banking states since they are able to expand through branch banking.

Other factors also influence the type of form a bank adopts such as banks' financial performance, capital structure, demographic characteristics, and state characteristics. Most small banks are unable to pursue a multi-bank holding company strategy due to budget constraints. Larger banks, larger in terms of assets, have greater resources at their disposal to pursue a multi-bank holding company strategy and to acquire other banks. While the number of branch banks is positively correlated with absolute bank size, there should not be an independent effect of number of branch banks on the founding and acquisition rates of multi-bank holding companies because unit banking states do not allow branch banking. Organization inertia increases as an organization ages due to the established traditions of organizational routines and practices (Hannan and Freeman 1989). Therefore, bank age should have a negative relateship with the founding of bank holding companies which create change in established practices and routines. How bank age should affect acquisition rates is unclear. However, bank age should be related to bank failure rates because of a "liability of newness" (Stinchcombe 1965). This implies that the failure rate of a bank should be highest in the early years of a banks existence.

Financial performance is expected to be an important influence on bank strategies. The lead banks of multi-bank holding companies are expected to be strong performers with above average returns on assets and equity. This should also hold for lead banks of one-bank holding companies. An attractive bank for a multi-bank holding company to acquire is a bank with a low equity to asset ratio (capitalization) and realizing moderate to low returns on assets (under-performing). The acquiring holding company is interested in buying established market share and goodwill, but at a reasonable price. Therefore, an acquiring bank is looking to purchase under-performing banks that show the potential for improvements in financial performance (Rose 1988; Koch 1988). A moderate to low return on assets provides a signal to the acquiring bank that financial performance could be improved. A low return on assets gives the acquiring bank holding company leverage to bargain down the acquisition price and to minimize acquisition premiums (the price paid above book value for goodwill). In addition, an acquiring holding company is interested in banks with a relatively low equity to asset ratio. This enhances the ability of the acquiring bank to use the assets of the acquired bank to secure low-cost financing for the stock buyout and achieve tax savings (Koch 1988). Using debt rather than shareholder equity to finance acquisitions is the preferred strategy to take advantage of the tax code. Therefore, lead banks of multi- and one-bank holding companies are expected to be strong performance banks in terms of their return on assets ratios, while acquired banks are expected to have low to moderate return on assets ratios. Also, lead banks of multi-bank holding companies are expected to be well capitalized in terms of their equity to assets ratios which would enhance their ability to generate favorable financing for their acquisitions, while acquired banks are expected to have relatively low capitalization ratios.

Shareholder returns are closely tied to a bank's capital structure as defined by its equity to asset ratio (Cole 1972; Koch 1988; Boyd and Graham 1993). A declining asset base places pressure on a banks' return on equity ratio by forcing a bank to earn higher returns on assets to maintain uniform shareholder returns. Banks can respond to a decreasing asset base by either increasing their earnings on assets by increasing efficiency or by expansion into non-bank, bank markets. I assume that bankers manage their banks as efficiently as possible and that increasing earnings on assets to offset shrinking asset markets is more difficult for banks to accomplish than increasing leverage through acquisition or expansion into non-bank, bank markets. On average, the lead banks of multi-bank holding companies are expected to have slack resources as evidenced by high equity to asset ratios and that the banks they acquire will have low to moderate equity to asset ratios.

In addition to bank characteristics, I control state characteristics as well. It is likely that multi-bank holding company founding and acquisition are higher in states with higher per capita income and a higher percentage of urban population. The greater the concentration of people in an urban market area increases the potential market share and reduces unit costs. On the other hand, the higher the per capita income of a state, the greater the base of affluent customers from which to draw. Since the number of units banks are greater in unit banking states, those regions of the country with more unit banking states should have higher founding and acquisition rates.

I perform a separate analysis of bank failures with the purpose of contrasting the characteristics of failed banks with other bank types. The United States economy was very volatile in the late 1970s and 1980s. High inflation and industrial relocation caused by large increases in energy prices, regional boom and bust cycles in real estate and energy markets, industrial restructuring caused by increased foreign competition, and stagnant agricultural markets created regional and national stresses on the economy which significantly impacted banking. The savings and loan banking industry collapsed in the mid-1980s and commercial bank failures approached Depression era numbers in the late 1980s. Research indicates that bank failures are more prominent among small banks than relatively large banks (Johnson and Johnson 1985). I hypothesize that multi-bank holding companies are not willing to acquire banks with a high risk of failure, and therefore, there should be a clear distinction between the characteristics of acquired banks and banks that fail. Failed banks are expected to be smaller banks with poor financial performance (very low return on assets and equity) while acquired banks are expected to be under-performing banks (low to moderate return on assets and equity) and of moderate size.

DATA AND METHODs

Data

The sources for the bank data are the Federal Reserve System's *Bank Holding Company File* and *Report of Income and Condition*. These data sources provide information on all commercial banks and bank holding companies operating in the United States. The Federal Reserve's bank holding company file provides the exact dates that bank holding company charters were issued and the dates when bank acquisitions were approved. The bank holding company file does not contain financial data on bank holding companies or their subsidiaries. The Federal Reserve's quarterly *Report of Income and Condition* contains detailed financial information on all commercial banks in the United States. Only data provided in the fourth quarter (end of year) editions of *Report of Income and Condition* for the years 1977-1988 are used in the study. Listings and dates of bank failures were obtained from the Federal Deposit Insurance Corporation's *Annual Report*. Because of the difference in the years covered by the Federal Reserve data sources, two separate models are estimated—one for 1956-1991 and the other 1978-1989. Note that for the 1978-1989 analysis I am lagging the financial data for 1977-1988 one year to account for backward looking decision-making processes. I assume that managers use recent past data in making decisions about future actions.

In addition to bank data, I gathered information population and income information on the states that banks are located. The source for state population and income data is the *Statistical Abstract of the United States* published annually by the Census Bureau. State population and per capita income data is from the 1960, 1970, 1980, and 1990 census reports. For analysis purposes, census estimates are assigned to the midpoints of ten year spans—1960 estimates for 1956-1965; 1970 estimates for 1966-1975; 1980 estimates for 1976-1985; and 1990 estimates for 1986-1991.

The explanatory variables for the analyses of bank holding company foundings and acquisitions are grouped into four categories—institutional effects, bank financial performance, bank characteristics, and control variables. A description of the independent variables by their abbreviated titles used in the tables are:

Institutions:

"branch state"—dummy variable for states that allow statewide branch
     banking.
"lim bran st"—dummy variable for states that allow limited branch banking.
"unit state"—excluded dummy variable for states that prohibit branch
     banking.
"fed. res. mem."—dummy variable for Federal Reserve member banks.
"bank type"—(for bank failure analysis only) 1) independent bank,
     2) one-bank holding company, 3) multi-bank holding company,
     4) acquired bank

Financial Performance:

"return on assets"—ratio of net income to total assets in constant 1991 dollars.

"return on equity"—ratio of net income to equity capital in constant 1991 dollars.

Bank Characteristics:

"bank age"—bank age in years.

"bank size"—total bank assets ($1000s) in constant 1991 dollars.

"# branches"—number of branch banks.

"capitalization"—ratio of equity capital to total assets in constant 1991 dollars.

"equity multiplier"—ratio of total assets to equity capital in constant 1991 dollars.

"bank type"—1) independent bank, 2) one-bank holding company, 3) lead bank of MBHC, 4) MBHC subsidiaries.

Controls:

"interest rate"—interest rate is approximated by an annual average of three month treasury bills.

"% st.pop.urb."—the percentage of a state's population that resides in a Standard Metropolitan Area (SMA).

"st.inc/cap."—a state's per capita income in constant 1987 dollars.

"oil state"—banks operating in Texas, Oklahoma, and Louisiana.

"region"—1) northeast, 2) south, 3)midwest, 4) west.

I employ a data structure which accounts for time-varying explanatory variables. The values for the variables interest rate, financial performance. and bank characteristics are updated annually. Values for state branch banking laws are adjusted to June 30th of the year that the laws change. All time-varying explanatory variables represent lagged values so that the value in a given year is the year-end value of the previous year.

A multi-bank holding company is defined as a corporation that controls twenty-five percent or more of the voting shares of at least two commercial banks. A multi-bank holding company is generally formed by a single commercial bank. However, some multi-bank holding companies have been founded by a coalition of banks, and therefore, have multiple lead banks. Being unable to distinguish between these two cases, all multi-bank holding companies are assumed for this analysis to have only one lead bank. It is believed that relatively few multi-bank holding companies have been founded by bank coalitions over the observation period.[1] If a bank holding company owns only one bank, it is classified as a one-bank holding company. The bank founding a holding company, either a one- or multi-bank holding company, is defined as the "lead bank."

The founding date of a multi-bank holding company is considered to be the date on which the holding company acquired its second bank. The twenty-six multi-bank holding companies formed prior to January 1, 1956 are excluded from the analysis. The population of commercial banks at risk of either founding a multi-bank holding company or being acquired are those commercial banks that have not previously been acquired by a bank holding company. A commercial bank is classified as acquired if a bank holding company or one of its direct subsidiaries controls a twenty-five percent interest in the bank. Banks acquired before January 1, 1956 have been excluded from the analysis.

Any commercial bank that has less than twenty-five percent of its stock held by a bank holding company is defined as an independent bank. If a bank is acquired by more than one bank holding company, the acquisition occurring earliest in time is the event of interest and subsequent acquisitions are ignored. If a commercial bank is acquired by more than one holding company simultaneously, the holding company founded at the earliest date is considered the acquiring company. Commercial banks chartered after January 1, 1956 are included in the data set. Banks that cease operations are censored on June 1 of the year that they cease operations. Censoring means that the bank is no longer included in the data set from the date of censoring to the end of the observation period. Commercial banks not experiencing an event, either multi-holding company founding or acquisition, by the end of the study period are right censored. Right censoring is a term referring to banks that experience no events of interest over the observation period.

To estimate the founding and acquisition rates of bank holding company, the start time for estimating founding and acquisition rates is either January 1, 1956 or January 1, 1978 depending on the time period being analyzed. If a bank was founded after these start times, the start time for these banks is the date the bank was chartered. All independent commercial banks are considered at risk of potentially founding a bank holding company or being acquired by a bank holding company. When analyzing the acquisition of independent banks by multi-bank holding companies, I am only considering first acquisitions. Once a bank has become part of a multi-bank holding company structure, its subsequent history is ignored. I do not study acquisitions of multi-bank holding companies or the selling of subsidiary banks after they are initially acquired by a MBHC.

A limitation of the 1978-1989 analysis is "left censoring." Since bank holding company foundings and acquisitions occurred before January 1, 1978 are not included, this data is left censored. Left censoring is a term applied to variables for which there is no information prior to the beginning date of the analysis. The loss of information due to excluded cases can introduce bias in the parameter estimates if prior history has a significant effect on the course of future events (Tuma and Hannan 1984:129). An inexact assessment of potential bias is evaluated by comparing the parameter estimates of the models for the two time periods—1956-1991 and 1978-1989. If the estimates of the two models are similar then the extent of the bias is not problematic.

Descriptive statistics and correlations for the dependent and explanatory variables are presented in Tables 4-2 through 4-5. In addition, I provide an numerical overview of banking events over the observation period in Tables 4-6 and 4-7.

Methods

Four event history models are designed to investigate the structural changes in commercial banking. In the first model, the founding rate of multi-bank holding companies is the dependent variable. In the second model, the dependent variable is the rate of bank acquisitions by multi-bank holding companies. The third model incorporates the founding rate of one-bank holding companies as the dependent variable. In the fourth model, the dependent variable is commercial bank failures. Since financial information on banks is available only for the period 1977-1988, there are two separate analyses performed. One, an analysis of the 1956-1991 period without bank financial variables, and a second covering the period 1978-1989. Note that the variables for financial performance and bank characteristics are lagged a year to take into account the assumption that bank managers make

Table 4-2. Descriptive Statistics: 1956-1991 Data.

	Mean	S.D.	Min.	Max.
Branch Bank State	0.20	0.42	0.00	1.00
Lim Branch Bank State	0.62	0.49	0.00	1.00
Unit Banking State	0.18	0.42	0.00	1.00
Fed. Res. Mem.	0.40	0.49	0.00	1.00
Failed Bank	0.12	0.32	0.00	1.00
% State Pop. Urban	64.89	18.19	12.78	99.19
State per Capita Inc.	11513	2761	4483	22083
Interest Rate	5.77	2.24	1.73	14.02
Region	2.35	0.85	1.00	4.00

N = 450451

****

Table 4-3. Descriptive Statistics: 1978-1989 Data.

	Mean	S.D.	Min.	Max.
Branch Bank State	0.22	0.41	0.00	1.00
Lim Branch Bank State	0.64	0.48	0.00	1.00
Unit Banking State	0.14	0.37	0.00	1.00
Fed. Res. Mem.	0.40	0.49	0.00	1.00
Failed Bank	0.13	0.34	0.00	1.00
% State Pop. Urban	67.43	17.84	18.33	99.19
State per Capita Inc.	13981	1915	9540	22083
Interest Rate	8.61	2.62	5.27	14.02
Region	2.41	0.84	1.00	4.00
Bank Age	59.13	37.47	0.13	189.00
Size (assets/1000s)	114085	547294	-100.48	3.4E-7
Log Assets	9.07	5.11	-4.61	17.34
# Branch Banks > 2	0.13	0.33	0.00	1.00
Capitalization	0.08	0.05	1.0E-3	1.00
Equity Multiplier	36.50	78.87	1.00	1000.00
Return on Assets (ROA)	0.85	1.85	-108.06	92.89
Return on Equity (ROE)	8.66	441.80	-1442.90	980.20
Oil State	0.17	0.38	0.00	1.00

N = 143540

Table 4-4. Zero-Order Correlations: 1956-1991 Data.

	(1)	(2)	(3)	(4)	(5)	(6)	(7)	(8)	(9)
1) Bran St	—								
2) Lim	St	-.64	—						
3) Unit St	-.24	-.61	—						
4) Fed Res	.08	-.10	.06	—					
5) Fail Bk	-.10	.02	.08	-.05					
6) %PopUrb	.12	-.09	-.02	.13	—				
7) St Inc	.09	.07	-.27	-.03	.41	—			
8) IntRate	.03	-.17	.22	.01	-.01	-.14	—		
9) Region	-.18	-.04	.12	-.15	-.15	.12	-.04	.02	—

N = 450451

****

Table 4-5. Zero-Order Correlations: 1978-1989 Data.

	(1)	(2)	(3)	(4)	(5)	(6)	(7)	(8)
1) Bran State	—							
2) Lim State	-.71	—						
3) Unit State	-.22	-.53	—					
4) Fed Res Mem	.08	-.11	.05	—				
5) Failed Bank	-.11	-.01	.12	-.03	—			
6) % Pop Urb	.22	-.16	-.06	.11	.02	—		
7) St Inc/Cap	.13	-.11	-.01	.05	-.06	.58	—	
8) Inter. Rate	-.02	-.01	.03	.03	.04	.01	-.32	—
9) Region	-.14	.03	.12	-.13	.05	-.10	.13	-.08
10) Bank Age	-.10	.15	-.09	-.01	-.09	-.18	.06	-.18
11) Log Assets	-.07	.07	-.02	-.15	-.03	.07	.06	.01
12) Capital.	-.01	.02	-.02	.01	-.13	.01	.03	-.02
13) Eq. Multi.	.09	-.09	.02	.03	.17	.02	-.02	-.02
14) ROA	-.01	.03	-.04	-.04	-.30	-.04	.02	.05
15) ROE	-.01	.02	-.03	-.02	-.07	-.01	-.01	.01
16) Branch Banks	.20	-.08	-.13	.05	-.06	.07	.01	-.01
17) Oil State	-.24	.12	.13	.09	.32	.14	-.23	-.01

	(9)	(10)	(11)	(12)	(13)	(14)	(15)	(16)	(17)
9) Region	—								
10) Bk Age	-.06	—							
11) Bk Size	-.07	.08	—						
12) Cap	-.03	-.01	-.06	—					
13) EM	.01	-.04	-.01	-.16	—				
14) ROA	-.05	.16	.02	.29	-.36	—			
15) ROE	-.02	.02	.01	.05	-.19	.15	—		
16) Branch	-.23	.13	.22	-.03	-.12	.01	.02	—	
17) Oil St	-.09	-.13	-.03	-.08	.10	-.19	-.02	-.10	—

N = 143540

Table 4-6. Tally of Events by Year in Commercial Banking, 1956-1991.

Year	MBHC Fnd.	Total MBHC	MBHC Acq.	Total Acq.	OBHC Fnd.	Indep. Fnd.	Bank Failures
pre-1956	35	35	310	310	n.a.	n.a.	n.a.
1956	2	37	3	313	69	84	2
1957	0	37	1	314	6	46	2
1958	1	38	11	325	10	63	4
1959	4	42	7	332	9	88	3
1960	0	42	10	342	23	93	1
1961	2	44	4	346	29	69	5
1962	3	47	13	359	29	128	1
1963	4	51	14	373	35	206	2
1964	7	58	9	382	51	206	6
1965	8	66	25	407	45	136	5
1966	11	77	61	468	47	82	7
1967	12	89	44	512	97	72	4
1968	12	101	32	544	134	65	3
1969	28	129	96	640	191	93	9
1970	48	177	179	819	189	128	6
1971	30	207	155	974	36	129	7
1972	50	257	229	1203	33	154	2
1973	50	307	298	1501	60	237	6
1974	44	351	254	1755	81	260	3
1975	27	378	121	1876	94	200	12
1976	21	399	89	1965	93	132	16
1977	28	427	90	2055	105	140	4
1978	25	452	82	2137	177	135	5
1979	33	485	97	2234	228	184	10
1980	42	527	124	2358	448	193	11
1981	68	595	174	2532	504	186	7
1982	109	704	237	2769	699	301	33
1983	159	863	252	3021	719	350	43
1984	241	1104	266	3287	671	390	78
1985	220	1324	203	3490	496	314	118
1986	186	1510	195	3685	341	243	143
1987	146	1656	127	3812	257	207	199
1988	126	1782	108	3920	223	223	218
1989	99	1881	107	4027	201	n.a.	205
1990	89	1970	88	4115	172	n.a.	160
1991	61	2031	67	4182	132	n.a.	114
Totals	2031	4182	6734	5537	1454		

Source: Board of Governors of the Federal Reserve System, Bank Holding Company File and Report of Income and Condition, 1977-1988. Federal Deposit Insurance Corporation, Annual Report.

Table 4-7. Tally of Banks by Bank Type and by State Branch Banking
Law as of December 31, 1989.

Branch Banking States

	Number	Percent
Independent Banks	1543	41%
One-Bank Holding Companies	1244	33%
Multi-Bank Holding Companies	322	9%
Subsidiaries of MBHCs	629	17%

Limited Branch Banking States

	Number	Percent
Independent Banks	2657	27%
One-Bank Holding Companies	4870	50%
Multi-Bank Holding Companies	859	9%
Subsidiaries of MBHCs	1387	14%

Unit Banking States

	Number	Percent
Independent Banks	496	13%
One-Bank Holding Companies	682	17%
Multi-Bank Holding Companies	839	22%
Subsidiaries of MBHCs	1884	48%

Source: Board of Governors of the Federal Reserve System, Bank
Holding Company File and Report of Income and Condition, 1977-1988.

decisions about future courses of action with information from the recent past which in this case is prior end-of-year information.

In this chapter, I analyze the transitions of independent banks to lead banks of multi-bank holding companies, to lead banks one-bank holding companies, to becoming subsidiaries of multi-bank holding companies, or to becoming failed banks. The appropriate statistical method to use when studying discrete state processes over time such as the transition of banks from state p to state z within the period t_0 - T is event history analysis (Tuma and Hannan 1984; Blossfeld, Hamerle and Mayer 1989). Since transition rates are non-negative, a log-linear model of transition rates is estimated taking the form

$$\log r(t) = -\beta'x + u$$

where r(t) is the transition rate, the x are vectors containing the values of explanatory variables, the βs are the estimates of the effects of the explanatory variables on transition rates, and u is the error term that captures the effects of omitted explanatory variables. This implies that

$$r(t) = e^{-\beta'x}e^{u}.$$

Note that the signs of the βs are negative because transition rates are calculated in terms of the time a case remains in state p before making a transition to state z. It follows that explanatory variables which increase the transition rate decrease the amount of time that a case is expected to remain in state p before making a transition to state z.

It is problematic to differentiate between banks founded before and after the 1956 and 1978 start times of the analyses performed. In order to take into account the event times for banks founded post-1956 and post-1978, I decided to estimate the models using a constant rate, exponential event history model. While it is entirely plausible that unobserved population heterogeneity and elapsed time have an effect on transition rates, the data structure precludes the estimation of models that take into account these effects.

Since the modeling of transition rates is a log-linear model, the anti-log of the explanatory variable coefficients is interpreted as a multiplier effect. By exponentiating the coefficients of continuous explanatory variables is interpreted as the percentage increase or decrease in the transition rate for a one unit increase in the explanatory variable. The exponentiation of dummy variables is interpreted as the percentage increase or decrease in transition rates for the presence of an attribute versus the absence of the attribute. The event history results presented in Tables 4-8 through 4-11 are the un-exponentiated transformed coefficients. I refer to the multiplier effect of explanatory variables on bank transition rates in the body of the paper which is the exponentiated coefficients.

The likelihood ratio test is an appropriate goodness-of-fit measure for the event history models (Kalbfleisch and Prentice 1980:48). The likelihood ratio test,

$$R(\theta) = -2(\log L_1 - \log L_2),$$

can be used to evaluate the comparative fit of nested event history models since the asymptotic distribution of $-2\log R(\theta)$ is chi-square with q degrees of freedom where q is the difference in the number of constraints between the models being evaluated.

FINDINGS

The event history models of multi-bank holding company founding rates are presented in Table 4-8. The results presented in the tables are untransformed. I present the exponentiated findings in this section which means that the estimates are interpreted as the proportionate change in the transition rate for a unit change in the explanatory variable. In other words, the effect of the explanatory variables is interpreted as a multiplier effect on the transition rate. In reporting the findings for the various models estimated, I will first report the 1956-1991 results, which are in the far right hand column of the tables, then I will report the 1978-1989 results.

As predicted state banking laws have a statistically significant effect on the founding rate of multi-bank holding companies. Over the period 1956-1991, the founding rate of multi-bank holding companies is 6.9 times higher in unit banking states than in branch banking states. The founding rate of multi-bank holding companies is 4.7 times higher in unit banking states than in limited branch banking states. Both of these results are statistically

Table 4-8. Founding Rates: Multi-Bank Holding Companies, 1978-1989
and 1956-1991. Exponential Event History Models.

	1978-1989 Models				'56-'91
	(1)	(2)	(3)	(4)	(A)
Intercept	-12.62**	-12.69**	-19.44**	-21.30**	-17.17**
Institutions					
Branch State	-1.66**	-1.67**	-2.19**	-2.52**	-1.93**
Lim.Bran.St.	-1.61**	-1.62**	-1.72**	-1.75**	-1.54**
Fed.Res.Mem.	0.20**	0.20**	-0.11	-0.12*	0.16**
Performance					
Return Assets	--	0.05**	0.02	0.02	--
Return Equity	--	3.1E-3**	0.01**	0.01**	--
Characteristics					
Bank Age	--	--	1.0E-3	-1.6E-3	--
Size (Assets)	--	--	0.65**	0.64**	--
Branch Banks	--	--	0.38**	0.38**	--
Capitalization	--	--	2.02*	1.71*	--
Equity Multipl.	--	--	-0.02**	-0.03**	--
Controls					
Interest Rate	--	--	--	0.02*	0.13**
State Pop.Urb.	--	--	--	-0.01**	-0.01**
State Income	--	--	--	2.1E-4**	3.1E-4**
Oil State	--	--	--	-0.21*	--
Region	--	--	--	-0.15	-0.34**
-2 LL Ratio	698.0**	29.1**	698.3**	134.7**	1748.1**
d.f.	3	2	5	5	7

** -- $p < .01$; * -- $p < .05$

1956-'91 -- N=17426; # Events 1758; Censored 448693
1978-'89 -- N=14277; # Events 1210; Censored 127866

significant. The findings support the hypothesis that the multi-bank holding company form is more likely in unit banking states since bank acquistions are a means of evading branch bank restrictions in these states. This evidence lends credence to the theoretical premise that bank strategies are framed within the context of state and federal branch banking laws.[2] In addition, Federal Reserve member banks have a 17 percent higher probability of founding a multi-bank holding company than non-Federal Reserve member banks. This finding is statistically significant.

All of the control variables have a statistically significant effect on the multi-bank holding company founding rate for the 1956-1991 period. An increase in the interest rate causes a large increase in the founding rate. This effect is due to the fact that interest rates were rising throughout most of the observation period at an increasing rate. Surprisingly, a percent increase in states' urban population ratio decreases the multi-bank holding company founding rate by 271 percent. For each $1,000 increase in a states' per capita income the founding rate of multi-bank holding companies increases by 36 percent. The negative sign for region indicates that the founding rate of multi-bank holding companies is higher in eastern and southern states than in midwestern and western states.

The results for the 1978-1989 period models are very similar to the 1956-1991 results. Return on assets does not have a statistically significant effect on the multi-bank holding company founding rate. Return on equity has a positive and statistically significant effect on the multi-bank holding company founding rate. A one percent increase in return on equity increases the founding rate by 23 percent. All the bank characteristic variables have a statistically significant effect except for bank age. Bank size, number of branch banks, and capitalization have positive effects on the multi-bank holding company founding rate, whereas, the equity multiplier variable has a negative effect. The effects of the control variables are very similar to the 1956-1991 findings. The founding rate of multi-bank holding companies is 23 percent lower in oil states compared to non-oil states.

The findings for the rate of bank acquisitions in the 1956-1991 period are presented in Table 4-9. The institutional effects on bank acquisition rates are all statistically significant. The acquisition rate in unit banking states is 7.2 time higher than it is in branch banking states and 6.2 times higher than it is in limited branch banking states. These findings support the hypothesis that the acquisitions of multi-bank holding companies are a means of branch

Table 4-9. Acquisition Rates: Multi-Bank Holding Companies, 1978-1989
and 1956-1991. Exponential Event History Models.

| | 1978-1989 Models | | | | '56-'91 |
Variables:	(1)	(2)	(3)	(4)	(A)
Intercept	-12.35**	-12.32**	-13.62**	-13.73	-14.31**
Institutions					
Branch State	-1.34**	-1.34**	-1.53**	-2.10**	-1.97**
Lim.Bran.St.	-1.54**	-1.54**	-1.54**	-1.71**	-1.82**
Fed.Res.Mem.	0.20**	0.19	0.15**	0.06	0.24**
Performance					
Return Assets	--	-0.03**	-0.03	-0.03*	--
Return Equity	--	-5.4E-4	-6.0E-5	-2.8E-4	--
Characteristics					
Bank Age	--	--	-0.01**	-0.01**	--
Size (Assets)	--	--	0.14**	0.08**	--
Branch Banks	--	--	0.43**	0.16	--
Capitalization	--	--	0.34	-0.27	--
Equity Multipl.	--	--	1.2E-3	1.6E-3	--
Controls					
Interest Rate	--	--	--	0.09**	0.12**
State Pop.Urb.	--	--	--	0.01**	7.0E-5
State Income	--	--	--	6.0E-5**	1.7E-4**
Oil State	--	--	--	-0.61**	--
Region	--	--	--	-0.54**	-0.55**
-2 LL Ratio	822.0**	5.6	129.4**	499.2**	4483.7**
d.f.	3	2	5	5	7

** -- $p < .01$; * -- $p < .05$
1956-1991 -- N=17426; # Events 3871, Censored 446580
1978-1989 -- N=14277; # Events 1711, Censored 127365

banking in unit banking states. Federal Reserve member banks are 31 percent more likely to be acquired than are non-Federal Reserve member banks.

All the control variables for the 1956-1991 period have a statistically significant effect on the acquisition rate except for the urban population ratio variable. An increase in the interest rate has a large, positive effect on the acquisition rate. An increase in states' per capita income by $1,000 increases the acquisition rate by 18 percent. The acquisition rate is higher in eastern and southern states than in midwestern and western states. All the acquisition rate findings are consistent with the multi-bank holding company founding rate results.

The institutional effects on bank acquisition rates in the 1978-1989 period are basically identical to the estimates for the 1956-1991 period. The acquisition rate in unit banking states is 8.2 times higher than it is in branch banking states and 5.5 times higher than it is in limited branch banking states. Both of these estimates are statistically significant. Whether a member bank of the Federal Reserve or not does not have a statistically significant effect on the acquisition rate. Return on assets has a negative, significant effect on the bank acquisition rate.[3] A one percent increase in return on assets reduces the acquisition rate by 2000 percent. This finding supports the contention that under-performing banks are acquisition targets. Return on equity does not have a statistically significant effect on the acquisition rate. Of the bank characteristic variables, only bank age and size have significant effects on the acquisition rate. The older the bank, the less likely it is to be acquired. The larger the bank the more likely it is too be acquired. The variables number of branch banks, capitalization, and equity multiplier do not have an effect on the acquisition rate. All of the control variables have a statistically significant effect on the acquisition rate, and they are similar to the 1956-1991 effects. The bank acquisition rate is 1.84 times lower in oil states than it is in non-oil states.

I now turn to the founding of one-bank holding companies in the 1956-1991 period which are presented in Table 4-10. The founding rate of one-bank holding companies is 23 percent higher in branch banking states compared to unit banking states and 227 percent higher in limited branch banking states compared to unit banking states. Both of the findings are statistically significant. These findings are in stark contrast to the results for multi-bank holding company founding and acquisition rates. Federal Reserve

Table 4-10. Founding Rates: One-Bank Holding Companies, 1978-1989 and 1956-1991. Exponential Event History Models.

| Variables: | 1978-1989 Nested Models | | | | '56-'91 |
	(1)	(2)	(3)	(4)	(A)
Intercept	-12.59**	-12.66**	-12.73**	-15.59**	-17.95**
Institutions					
Branch State	0.29**	0.29**	0.28**	0.52**	0.21**
Lim Bran St.	0.78**	0.77**	0.81**	0.95**	0.82**
Fed.Res.Mem.	0.03	0.03	0.03	0.03	-0.07**
Performance					
Return Assets	--	0.04**	0.06**	0.06**	--
Return Equity	--	3.0E-3**	0.01**	0.01**	--
Characteristics					
Bank Age	--	--	-3.3E-3**	-3.4E-3**	--
Size (Assets)	--	--	0.10**	0.15**	--
Branch Banks	--	--	0.05	0.07	--
Capitalization	--	--	-5.21**	-4.47**	--
Equity Multipl.	--	--	-0.04**	-0.03**	--
Controls					
Interest Rate	--	--	--	0.12**	0.22**
State Pop.Urb.	--	--	--	-0.02**	-0.01**
State Income	--	--	--	1.4E-4**	2.7E-4**
Oil State	--	--	--	0.38**	--
Region	--	--	--	0.06**	0.08**
-2 LL Ratio	347.3**	91.9**	212.6**	627.6**	9296.6**
d.f.	3	2	5	5	7

** -- $p < .01$; * -- $p < .05$
1956-1991 -- N=17426; # Events 6533; Censored 432653
1978-1989 -- N=12825; # Events 4518; Censored 83433

member banks are 7 percent less likely to form a one-bank holding company than are non-Federal Reserve member banks, and this effect is statistically significant. The effect of Federal Reserve membership on the founding rate of one-bank holding companies is also opposite its effect on multi-bank holding company founding and acquisition rates.

Each of the control variables have a statistically significant effect on the founding rate of one-bank holding companies. An increase in interest rates has a large positive effect on the founding rate of one-bank holding companies. A one percent increase in the urban population of a state decreases the founding rate of one-bank holding companies by 272 percent. For each $1,000 increase in a states' per capita income there is a corresponding 31 percent increase the founding rate of one-bank holding companies. The founding rate of one-bank holding companies is 8 percent higher in midwestern and western states compared to eastern and southern states.

Once again, the findings for the 1978-1989 period are very similar to the findings for the 1956-1991 period. The founding rate of one-bank holding companies is 68 percent higher in branch banking states than it is in unit banking states. The founding rate of one-bank holding companies is 2.6 times higher in limited branch banking states than it is in unit banking states. Both of these finding are statistically significant. Federal Reserve membership does not have a statistically significant effect on the founding rate of one-bank holding companies. Examining the effects of financial performance on one-bank holding company foundings in the 1978-1989 period, it is apparent that one-bank holding companies are founded by banks with above average financial performance in terms of return on assets and return on equity. Both return on assets and return on equity have a large, positive effect on the one-bank holding company founding rate, and both results are statistically significant. Federal Reserve membership does not have a statistically significant effect on the founding rate of one-bank holding companies.

Bank age has a negative effect on the one-bank holding company founding rate. In other words, older banks are more likely to found one-bank holding companies. Bank size in terms of assets has a positive and statistically significant effect on the founding rate of one-bank holding companies. The number of branch banks does not have a statistically significant effect on foundings. The capital structure findings are illuminating. The higher a banks capitalization ratio, the lower the founding rate of one-bank holding companies. An increase in the equity multiplier decreases the founding rate. Both of these effects are statistically significant. Both of the capital structure variables have a large effect on the founding rate of one-bank holding companies. These two findings, coupled with the financial performance findings, indicate the lead banks of one-bank holding companies have strong financial performance with textbook capital structure profiles. Shareholders receive a maximum of returns (low equity to asset ratio), yet the bank is not leveraged to the extent that great risk in incurred (low asset to equity ratio). Overall, the combined effects of financial performance and capital structure suggest that the strongest banks in terms of financial performance are the most likely to found one-bank holding companies. With the finding that one-bank holding company foundings are more likely to occur in branch and limited branch banking states, it is possible to make arguments that one-bank holding companies are founded as both an offensive strategy (for product diversification) and a defensive strategy (to prevent acquisition). The founding rate is 46 percent higher in oil states than in non-oil states. All the control variables have a statistically significant effect on the one-bank holding company founding rate for the 1978-1989 period and are very similar to the 1956-1991 findings.

In addition to the analysis of multi-bank holding company and one-bank holding company founding and acquisition rates, I include an analysis of bank failures which is presented in Table 4-11. The purpose of this analysis is to contrast the dynamics of bank failure to bank holding company events. It is obvious from reviewing the findings that bank failures were much higher in unit banking states than in branch or limited branch banking states over the observation periods. Relatively young, independent banks with low return on assets and low capitalization have the highest failure rates. The low return on assets coupled with the low capitalization ratio indicates that banks that failed over the observation period were banks willing to assume great risk. These findings produce suggest potential moral hazard possibly encouraged by the availability of deposit insurance. Research has indicated that bank failures in the 1980s were caused primarily by banks willing to assume great risk by making poor quality loans and by being under-capitalized. The reason banks were able to assume the high levels of risk and still attract depositors was the protection of depositors by federal deposit insurance. The failure rate of banks in oil states is 3.9 times greater than the

Table 4-11. Commercial Bank Failure Rates: 1977-1989 and
1956-1991. Event History Models.[a]

| Variables: | 1978-1989 Nested Models | | | | '56-'91 |
	(1)	(2)	(3)	(4)	(A)
Intercept	-90.55**	-103.94**	-105.10**	-159.40**	-184.99**
Institutions					
Branch St.	-1.73**	-1.15**	-1.58**	-1.20**	-0.58**
Lim Bran St.	-1.22**	-1.26**	-1.62**	-1.14**	-0.38**
Fed.Res.Mem.	2.0E-3	-0.31**	-0.31**	-0.14	-0.18*
Bank Type	--	--	-1.05**	-0.53**	-0.76**
Performance					
R.O.A.	--	-0.32**	-0.21**	-0.22**	--
R.O.E.	--	2.1E-5	3.3E-5	1.6E-5	--
Characteristics					
Bank Age	--	--	-0.01**	-0.01**	--
Size (Assets)	--	--	-1.5E-7	-1.1E-7	--
Branch Banks	--	--	-0.03	-0.04	--
Capitalization	--	--	-0.13**	-0.12**	--
Equity Multi.	--	--	-1.2E-4	7.7E-5	--
Controls					
Interest Rate	--	--	--	1.11**	0.19**
St. Pop. Urb.	--	--	--	0.01**	8.9E-4
State Income	--	--	--	-1.1E-4**	-6.4E-5**
Oil State	--	--	--	1.36**	--
Region	--	--	--	0.30**	0.20**
Scale	0.14**	0.12**	0.12**	0.08**	0.16**
-2 LL Ratio	343.6**	1097.1**	307.9**	1340.4**	--
d.f.	3	2	6	5	--

** -- $p < .01$; * -- $p < .05$
1978-'89 -- N=17771; # Events 1452, Censored 16319
1956-'91 -- N=14108; # Events 965, Censored 13143
[a] Weibull distribution.

bank failure rate in non-oil states.[4] The 1956-1991 and 1978-1989 models of bank failures are very similar, but the effects are enhanced in the later period which is consistent with the fact that bank failures were at very low rates until the late 1970s.

DISCUSSION AND SUMMARY

In the 1950s, commercial banks experienced a fourteen percent reduction in the market share of financial assets that they controlled (Table 2-1). The reduction in the market share of financial assets controlled by commercial banks was caused by increasing competition in financial markets. Credit unions, savings and loan associations, finance companies, mutual funds, and pension funds were all growing in the 1950s and taking a slice of market share in financial assets from commercial banks. The reduction in market share of assets controlled by commercial banks caused by increasing competition within the financial services industry provoked among commercial banks concerning their long-term stability (Kaufman 1994). To protect their interests, commercial bankers began a search for growth strategies to counter the increased competition coming from other sectors of the financial services industry. By the mid-1960s, two growth strategies began to be actively pursued by commercial bankers, the formation of multi-bank and one-bank holding companies.

The findings reported in this chapter clearly indicate that multi-bank and one-bank holding company foundings and acquisitions are systematic in that there is a distinct pattern in their distribution across branch banking regimes. The results support the contention that banks design strategies and adopt particular bank forms in response to institutional, resource, and economic conditions. The strategic response to constraints on branch banking opportunities in unit banking states is the formation of multi-bank holding companies. This strategy enables banks to pursue branch banking opportunities through the acquisition of independent banks in those states that strictly prohibit branch banking. In this manner, commercial banks in unit banking states can achieve market growth and market diversification in lieu of branch banking restrictions.

Budget constraints also play a significant role in the ability of organizations to change form and to adopt acquisition strategies (Hannan and

Freeman 1989; Haveman 1993). Commercial banks with potential slack resources, as measured by above average return on asset and equity ratios and above average capitalization, are the banks most likely to be lead banks of multi-bank and one-bank holding companies. In contrast, acquired banks have somewhat less than average return on assets and equity ratios and basically average capitalization profiles. On the other hand, failing banks have low return on assets and capitalization ratios.

The results presented in Tables 4-8 through 4-11 present a picture of commercial banks as strategically pursuing growth trajectories consistent with the prevailing constraints imposed by bank branch banking laws. The results of the two event history models for multi-bank holding company foundings (1956-1991 and 1978-1989) are very similar and lend support to the hypothesis that multi-bank holding company foundings are more likely to occur in unit banking states where the incentives for the strategic use of multi-bank holding company bank form are greatest. The founding rate of multi-bank holding companies is more than 5 times greater in unit banking states than in either branch or limited branch banking states. These findings are consistent with prior organizational research which links the adoption of innovative, organizational forms to externally imposed institutional constraints (Fligstein 1985, 1990). Innovative organizational strategies are more likely to be initiated by those organizational actors with the most to gain from the new practices.

The founding rate of one-bank holding companies is greater in branch and limited branch banking states compared to unit banking states. These findings are exactly the reverse of the findings for the founding and acquisition rates of multi-bank holding companies. These findings can be interpreted to mean that the one-bank holding company form is both a defensive strategy to protect against potential acquisition by predator banks and an offensive strategy for diversifying financial products and services.

The very large, negative effect of capitalization on one-bank holding company foundings reported in Table 4-10 is interesting. Many older, well-established banks of moderate size are family owned or owned by a few, large shareholding families who have controlled and managed the bank over generations. These family shareholdings are not marketed on exchanges, and hence, the market value of the stock is indeterminate which results in the book evaluation of bank equity to be much lower than the actual market value[5] (Koch 1988; Personal Interview 1995). This would explain the low capitalization ratio of one-bank holding companies. It is quite plausible that relatively large and profitable family controlled banks would have the greatest interest in maintaining control of their banks, and therefore, to form a one-bank holding company as a defensive strategy against acquisition attempts (Austin 1989). This interpretation is consistent with merger and acquisition research which has found a lower acquisition rate of owner controlled firms (Palmer et al 1987, 1995).

It is interesting to note that the effects of financial performance variables are basically the same on the founding rates of one-bank holding companies and multi-bank holding companies. In both cases it is the relatively strong performing banks that form multi-bank and one-bank holding companies. In contrast, a decrease in the return on assets ratio increases the likelihood that a bank will be acquired. These findings suggest that large, strong performance banks that form multi-bank holding companies are acquiring under-performing banks. This can be interpreted to mean that profitable banks are looking for relatively good buys with minimum premiums on book value. Also, it indicates that banks with relatively strong management and slack resources acquire under-performing banks with the expectation of realizing increased returns by improving the performance of the acquired banks. The financial performance of the acquired banks can be improved through the achievement of scale economies and through a reduction in unit costs with the realization of personnel and technology synergies.

These conclusions do not agree with a managerialist explanation of mergers and acquisitions. The managerial perspective predicts that large under-performing firms acquire profitable, well capitalized firms (Mueller 1986). However, the consolidation occurring in commercial banking is not exactly comparable to contemporary merger movements occurring in manufacturing and industry. For one thing, mergers and acquisitions in commercial banking are occurring for the first time. Whereas mergers in manufacturing and industry have been occurring for over a hundred years. For another, mergers and acquisitions in commercial banking are of the market extension variety rather than the horizontal variety. Horizontal mergers are designed to decrease market competition and are sure to capture the attention of anti-trust regulators. Market extension mergers are designed for growth into new markets and do not disrupt the balance of competition.

In conclusion, the analysis of bank holding company foundings and acquisitions clearly demonstrates the degree of change that is occurring in the structure of commercial banking in the United States. The choice under constraint explanation for the changes in commercial banking provides a good explanation for variations in the emerging structure of commercial banking. The institutional constraints of state and federal restrictions on branch banking and the federal segmentation of the financial services industry clearly appear to be key motivating factors in explaining the particular characteristics of change which is transforming commercial banking in the United States.

NOTES

1. The CEO of a bank holding company I interviewed stated that his holding company was founded by three moderately sized banks to offset the statewide growth of large urban banks in his state. It is was initially believed that the three banks would be equal partners in the new holding company, but the plan proved problematic since "it required the meeting of three independent minds to avoid personality conflicts." However, the Independent Bankers Association in the mid-1990s was promoting the idea of two or three relatively small banks forming a holding company as a defensive strategy against acquisition by larger bank holding companies.

2. Since unit bank states are the omitted category, a concern is that the large number of banks and events in unit states would generate spurious inferences resulting from population heterogeneity. However, many unit banking states changed their laws to limited branch banking laws and these are the states with the greatest number of banks and events. Overall, I am confident in the validity of the inferences being made.

3. Keep in mind that these results are somewhat biased by the inclusion of lead banks of multi-bank holding companies formed by a coalition of independent banks. The extent of the bias is unknown, but in lieu of the finding that lead banks of multi-bank holding companies are strong performers the bias is expected to be upward. It is reasonable to assume that the financial performance effects are actually somewhat less than those reported.

4. The oil states are Oklahoma, Texas, and Louisiana. Approximately 40 percent of all bank failures occurred in these three states in the 1980s and accounted for over 45 percent of all assets of failed banks.

5. The large, profitable, family bank scenario was described to me in an interview. In the case of the interview, a multi-bank holding company was formed and the value of stock was established by a Wall Street auditing firm and listed on a stock exchange. The motivation was for family members to ascertain market value

and have the opportunity to realize market value by selling shares through public offering on the stock exchange.

CHAPTER 5

Comparative Analysis of Bank Financial Performance across Bank Forms and State Branch Banking Regimes

The proliferation of bank holding companies is an interesting organizational phenomenon. The consensus among organizational researchers is that the holding company form is less than optimal when compared to more centralized organizational forms such as the unified or multi-divisional form (Chandler 1962:30-35, 1977:334-36; Williamson 1975:143-44, 1985:280-84). To illuminate why the multi-bank holding company form has been successful, a comparative analysis of the financial performance of banks by type of bank form and by type of state branch banking law over the 1978 to 1988 observation period is performed. The holding company form may be a less than optimal organizational form, but in lieu of state constraints on branch banking, the formation of a bank holding company may be a better option than remaining an independent bank.

In providing a theoretical model for evaluating bank financial performance, a critique of the traditional decision-making model from micro-economic theory is first presented, and a constrained choice decision-making model that explicitly takes into account the effects of the external institutional environment is offered in its place. From the partial adjustment decision-making model, testable hypotheses are derived to explain the diffusion of the multi-bank holding company form in terms of differentials in bank financial performance across bank forms and branch banking regimes. The partial adjustment model is premised on the notion that decision-makers are unable to fully attain goals due to constraints beyond their control.

Constraints on the achievement of performance strategies can come from external factors such as formal and informal institutions and economic conditions or from internal factors such as inertia. Therefore in lieu of external or internal constraints, short-term performance is evaluated in terms of partial adjustments toward long-term performance criteria.

As has often been noted in the sociological literature, institutional arrangements often result in unintended consequences. While Depression era federal banking laws were designed with the explicit intention of promoting a safe and sound banking system by limiting competition, Tables 2-1 and 2-2 illustrate how the incentives produced by the banking laws of the 1930s actually increased competition in financial service markets which created a potential threat to the long-term viability of many commercial banks. Within this context, commercial bankers began to see a need for strategies to counter their decreasing market share in deposits and loans (Eccles 1982). This was particularly true for bankers operating in unit and limited branch banking states who have less latitude to pursue growth options than do bankers in branch banking states, and therefore, would be more likely to initiate innovative growth strategies.

In unit and limited branch banking states the financial fortunes of a bank are closely tied to the economic fortunes of the community where they are located. When a community experiences business cycle downturns, the negative effect on banks is likely to be aggravated in unit and limited branch banking states since bank performance is more closely tied to local business conditions. The smaller the geographic market, the greater the effects of local market conditions on bank performance. If the economic conditions are favorable in a small geographic market, banks will prosper. But if economic conditions in a local market erode, banks will suffer if they are strictly limited to that local market. Banks operating in extensive geographic markets rather than solely in local markets are able to hedge the risks related to local business cycles.

Commercial banking is particularly susceptible to the agency problems of adverse selection and moral hazard, and these agency problems are accentuated by fluctuations in the business cycle (Kaufman 1992; Mishkin 1992). Downturns in the business cycle and prolonged economic crisis generate increased uncertainty in banking by making it more difficult for lenders to screen good from bad credit risks. With declining economic conditions, loan defaults increase causing a decrease in revenues and an increase in costs. In addition, those most in need of loans during economic downturns are those with the least ability to repay. To offset decreasing revenues and increasing costs, bankers experience pressure to make loans to generate revenues but at higher interest rates to compensate for the greater risk incurred due to depressed economic conditions. Good credit risks are least likely to be willing to pay the higher interest rates on loans which increases the percentage of poor risks in the pool of potential borrowers. These conditions create a situation where bankers are more likely to make adverse selections in their loan decisions. In addition, incentives created by federal deposit insurance give rise to the problem of moral hazard on the part of banks facing financial difficulties. Since bank depositors are protected by deposit insurance, bank managers are willing to assume greater risks in order to generate higher returns. This is especially the case if they are experiencing substantial short term losses due to depressed economic conditions.

The causes of financial crisis in banking are steep fluctuations in interest rates, unanticipated declines in the price level, increases in uncertainty caused by recessions, and prolonged stock market declines (Mishkin 1992:178-83). Particularly salient in the late 1970s and early 1980s were the effects of extremely high inflation and interest rates. With the introduction of small denomination money market instruments in the 1970s—which became very popular as investors attempted to keep pace with inflation—commercial bankers experienced substantially higher costs in keeping and attracting depositors. Money market rates were much higher than the regulated interest rates set by the Federal Reserve Board and effectively put an end to interest rate ceiling on deposits. In 1980, Congress passed legislation which began a phase-out of Regulation Q, interest rate ceilings on deposits for commercial banks and saving and loan banks. Interest rates on loans rose in conjunction with the increased interest rates on certificates of deposit which increased the probability of adverse selection and moral hazard.

In addition to the aforementioned economic factors confronting banks, significant regional financial crises occurred in the 1980s. The auto and steel industries collapsed in the early 1980s affecting steel producing states of the Midwest and Northeast; oil prices collapsed in the mid-1980s affecting oil producing states; farm prices also collapsed in the mid-1980s affecting Midwestern states; and real estate markets collapsed in the mid- to late-1980s in many regions of the country most notably in the Northeast, Texas, and California. These volatile economic conditions severely taxed the ability of many banks to respond in a timely and appropriate manner which led to a broad destabilization of the banking industry.

The volatile economic environment of the late 1970s and 1980s coupled with changes in the structure of financial markets resulted in a banking crisis by the mid-1980s. The savings and loan industry collapsed, and an extraordinary number of commercial bank failed (see Table 4-6). However, some banks fared relatively better than others. It is to be expected that those banks with the greatest latitude in diversifying risks were the banks that best weathered the storm. Theoretically, banks in branch banking states and multi-bank holding companies in unit and limited branch banking states would be the winners.

Economists, when analyzing the financial performance of firms, tend to focus solely on the marginal price characteristics of the firm's production function and to largely ignore the effects of the external institutional environment. Economic theory postulates that a firm's profitability is equal to total revenue minus total cost. To maximize profits managers perform marginal analysis of input costs and output revenues.[1] The optimal level of output to maximize profits, given market prices for both inputs and outputs, is determined by taking the first and second derivatives of the following marginal profit equation,

$$\frac{dP}{dx} = \frac{dp(x)}{dx} - \frac{dC}{dx} = 0. \qquad (1)$$

where P is the level of profit, p is the price of the product, x is the quantity produced, p(x) is the total revenue, and C is the total cost of production which includes both fixed and variable costs. Since market prices are assumed fixed for both inputs and outputs, the optimum level of production is the only strategic factor which the manager has to consider. Since it is assumed that the action of a single firm does not influence market behavior, the economic agents of this simplified model are operating in a world of complete information. The economic model of profit maximization does not conform with real world conditions or with real world economic behavior because economic behavior is not as tractable as the profit maximization model implies. The external environment of the firm is not benign due to diffuse competitive strategies and to unforeseen economic events which limit the capacity of managers to accurately process information and plan for contingencies. In addition to limits on information, managerial action is often constrained by institutional demands comprised of formal rules and informal traditions that are both internal and external to the firm. When information and institutional constraints are added to the profit maximization model, managers and owners become "intendedly rational, but only limited so" (Simon 1976: xxviii).

Rather than assuming the institutional environment as a given or benign, it is important to recognize the dynamic nature of the interaction between institutions and rational economic agents when explaining or predicting economic behavior. Bankers are perceived as strategic actors who respond to the structure of incentives (payoffs and opportunity costs) generated by the mix of regulations and economic conditions at any particular point in time. Institutional effects in the form of branch banking laws, interest rate regulations, and information constraints were significant in the turbulent economic environment of the 1970s and 1980s. In essence, the geographic and market constraints imposed on commercial banks by state and federal banking laws threatened the long-term viability of many banks. It is within this context of increased competition in financial markets that commercial banks began the search for growth strategies.

I treat banks as corporate actors who are endowed with behavioral characteristics analogous to human actors. Therefore, I assume that commercial banks make decisions and act. The behavioral assumption underlying commercial bank decision-making processes can be formally represented as

$$A = p(V) * I,$$

where A is action taken, V is the value of outcomes, p is the probability (objective or subjective) of attaining desired outcomes, and I is the institutional framework. In other words, banks' decisions concerning competitive strategies are determined by the interaction of rational calculation and banking laws and regulations. Since it is further assumed that bank managers are charged with the responsibility of maximizing shareholder wealth, it is expected that the diffusion of the bank holding companies form is coupled with improved financial performance in terms of greater returns on assets and equity. In addition, I expect the financial performance of banks to be conditional on state branch banking laws.

The central hypothesis is that the diffusion of the multi-bank holding company form is positively related to the improvements in the financial performance of their subsidiaries in comparison to independent banks in non-branch banking states. This may not be true in branch banking states. Independent banks in branch banking states had the opportunity to expand operations into desired banking markets throughout the state, and thereby, to have achieved economies of scale and scope.

Subsidiaries of bank holding companies are able to out-perform independent banks because the holding company form provides greater decision-making flexibility to pursue adaptive strategies. This should be particularly true in unit and branch banking states. The key point I make is that the financial performance of commercial banks in the 1980s is not solely a consequence of volatile economic conditions but is also a reflection of the interaction between bank forms and state branch banking laws. Therefore, some of the variance in financial performance among individual banks in the 1978-1989 period can be explained in terms of bank strategies as evidenced by differentials in bank structure across types of branch banking regimes.

Following the lead of Chandler (1962), I assume that bank structure follows strategy. Bank managers routinely devise and update strategies in response to periodic performance evaluations. Organizational structures evolve as adaptive solutions to specific problems that arise. Not all bankers confront the same problems nor desire the same objectives due primarily to institutional and budgetary constraints. The constrained choice decision-making model is an appropriate model to apply in explaining the diffusion of the multi-bank holding company form.[2] Banks devise competitive strategies in accordance with regulatory and budgetary constraints with the goal of maintaining acceptable levels returns. However, due to uncertainty created by regulatory constraints and incomplete information regarding the economic environment, banks are unable to completely realize long-term objectives in the short-term. Therefore, banks are expected to be involved in a continuous decision-making process of evaluating and updating short-term performance standards in terms of long-range objectives.

The desired level of bank performance is a function of some set of conditions, X, such that

$$P^*(t) = \beta' X(t) + u(t), \tag{2}$$

where $P^*(t)$ is the performance goal, and $u(t)$ is the influence of unaccounted factors. The partial adjustment model is premised on the assumption that banks are goal oriented, but because of constraints such as inertia, banking regulations, contractual obligations, et cetera, short-term performance is evaluated in terms of incremental adjustments toward longer-range performance goals. Bank managers are expected to periodically evaluate and adjust their short-term plans to account for the difference between actual performance and projected goals. Banks, just as other organizations, evaluate their present performance in terms of past performance. Also, it is fair to assume that managers and shareholders evaluate their performance in comparison to the performance of similar banks. Since the goal-setting process is based on a combination of long- and short-term criteria, it is expected that bankers attempt to attain long-term objectives in short-term increments. This is particularly salient for multi-bank holding companies in non-branch banking states as they formulate acquisition strategies. In other words, short-term banking behavior is perceived as a process of continuously making incremental adjustments toward longer range goals such that

$$P(t) - P(t-1) = r[P^*(t) - P(t-1)], \qquad (3)$$

where $P(t) - P(t-1)$ is the actual change over the observation period, $P^*(t) - P(t-1)$ is the desired change over the observation period, and r, $0 < r \leq 1$, is an adjustment parameter for each period.

Equation 3 postulates that change in performance in any given time period t is a fraction r of the desired change for that period. A r of 1 signifies that observed performance adjusts completely to the desired level of performance in each time period. On the other hand, a r of 0 means that nothing is changing since performance at time t is the same as performance at time $t-1$. By rearranging terms Equation 3 can be written as

$$P(t) = rP^*(t) + (1 - r)[P(t-1)]. \qquad (4)$$

Equation 4 demonstrates that observed performance at time t is a weighted average of the performance goal at time t and the observed performance in the previous time period. Substitution of Equation 2 into Equation 4 gives

$$P(t) = r\beta'X(t) + (1 - r)[P(t-1)] + ru(t). \tag{5}$$

The coefficient of adjustment (1 - r) estimates the percentage of adjustment between observed and projected performance in a given time period. Equation 5 is the short-term position, and Equation 2 represents the long-term performance goal. Once Equation 5 is estimated and the adjustment coefficient, r, is obtained from P(t-1), it is easy to derive the long-term function by simply dividing through by (1 - r).

The target (P*) is the level of return on assets and equity toward which owners and managers of commercial banks are striving to maintain. I argue that in unit and limited branch banking states independent banks have not achieved optimal size nor achieved optimal markets. Therefore, banks in unit and limited branch banking states which are acquired by multi-bank holding companies are viewed as moving toward higher rates of return on assets and equity through the realization of scale and scope economies. This should not hold for acquired banks in branch banking states since these banks have had the opportunity to achieve growth through branch banking and should have achieved economies of scale and scope prior to holding company formation or acquisition. In branch banking states, it is the single-bank holding companies which should be moving toward new targets of return on assets and equity as they seek profitable diversification opportunities and achieve synergies accruing from economies of scope. Independent banks in branch banking states are expected to perform as well as, if not better than, the lead banks of multi-bank holding companies or their subsidiaries. This is predicted because the managerial resources of the lead bank of the holding company structure are diluted through the process of consolidating bank acquisitions within the holding company structure. This diminishes the managerial capabilities of the lead banks of the multi-bank holding company structure.

The adoption of the bank holding company form is a firm level innovation designed to increase shareholder returns under adverse market conditions created by the interaction of changing financial markets and legal constraints on bank growth and diversification opportunities. The bank holding company strategy was not designed to maximize shareholder returns or to maximize the efficient utilization of assets in absolute terms, but a strategy designed to enhance survival prospects and to enable shareholders to realize competitive returns on their bank investments. Commercial banks operating in unit and limited branch banking states are confronted with limited options in improving their return on assets and equity ratios. The multi-bank holding company option, whether through acquisition or being acquired, provides shareholders and managers the opportunity achieve scale and scope economies, and thereby, improve their performance.

Many bank researchers conclude that scale economies are achieved at a relatively modest bank size (Clark 1988; Rose 1988; Humphrey 1990; Mishkin 1993), and that diseconomies of scale exist for the largest banks (Berger and Humphrey 1990). The general consensus of this body of research concludes that significant economies of scale exist for small banks with less than $100 million in deposits but that economies are exhausted in the $100-150 million range. The findings regarding scope economies is not as clear. Scope economies are realized by bank holding companies through synergies generated by the application of management and technological resources to multiple banking tasks. The synergies produced by the bank holding company reduce unit costs by maximizing the utilization of banking resources through the elimination of duplications in expenditures on technologies and managerial resources. It follows that multi-bank holding companies should realize significant scope economies within their bank network (Koch 1988).

A common argument in support of independent local banks is that local bankers can better assess loan risks. This argument is not as salient with the advent of computerized, information systems tied into regional and national credit rating services. Bank holding companies can attain synergies throughout their extensive banking networks by investing in state-of-the-art, information systems to facilitate the timely assessment of credit risks at low unit costs. Also, bank holding companies are able achieve asset diversification through the offering of additional financial services, as well as, through geographic market diversification which creates hedges against fluctuations in local business cycles. Small, independent banks are unable to hedge their investment portfolios as effectively and are more susceptible to adverse effects of downturns in local economies. Research on bank failures in the 1930s conclude that small, local banks are more prone to failure during economic downturns than large, diversified banks (Fisher 1961).

The predicted positive relationship between scale economies and improved financial performance runs contrary to many research findings on merger and acquisitions in the post-WWII era. A large body of research on the financial performance of conglomerates suggests that the conglomerate form is adopted for reasons other than profit maximization or the realization of scale economies (Mueller 1986a, 1986b; Fligstein 1985, 1990; Davis et al. 1992, 1994; Palmer et al. 1993, 1994). Managerial theory and research suggests that a primary cause of merger and acquisition activity is a desire for firm growth, rather than greater firm efficiency, because it has been found that managers' compensation is more closely tied to organizational size than to profitability (Marris 1964; Mueller 1986:82). This body of research attributes conglomerate merger and acquisition activity to the desire on the part of managers for growth (Mueller), power networks (Palmer et al.), or the elaboration of normative organizing models such as marketing or finance conceptions of control (Fligstein and Davis et al.) rather than the quest to improve financial performance. But regardless of how persuasive and appealing these arguments appear on the surface, the arguments ultimately rest on self-interest and strategies. Enduring power and normative relations are premised on a requirement that the needs of affected interests be met (Homans 1974). It follows that if the conglomerate form has not proved a successful strategy, then it is to be expected that the form would be abandoned. Organizational research has duly noted that conglomerates who are not producing satisfactory returns for their investors—even though they possess great power and normative legitimacy—are being challenged by a deconglomeration movement initiated by capital markets (Davis and Stout 1992; Davis, Diekmann, and Tinsley 1994).

Fligstein (1985, 1990) argues that the ascendancy of the finance conception of control by finance managers within Fortune 500 companies provided the thrust for the firm-as-portfolio model as exhibited by the conglomerate corporate form. Large corporations began to adopt the firm-as-portfolio model in the late 1940s in response to anti-trust constraints on vertical and horizontal growth strategies. Fligstein's results are consistent with the logic of the choice under constraint hypothesis I offer for adoption of the bank holding company strategy. However, Fligstein does not infer a rational actor model in explaining the rise of the conglomerate form. Instead he applies a cognitive theory premised on the legitimation of normative organizing models as evidenced by the number of financial managers, as opposed to the number of marketing executives, in control of conglomerate firms. Davis et al. (1992, 1994) embraces a similar theoretical strategy in explaining the de-legitimation of the conglomerate form in the 1980s. While denying the relevance of rational calculation and profit maximization, both Fligstein and Davis explicitly state that the merger events they investigated were successful in promoting the interests of finance managers and financial markets respectively. Fligstein's analysis of financial performance clearly indicates a non-negative effect on profits for all types of mergers and acquisitions except for vertical and multi-national mergers in the period 1948-1968 (Fligstein 1990:347-48). By categorically claiming that the conglomerate strategy of the 1960s was a failure in terms of optimizing shareholder returns, this body of research obfuscates the rich intricacies of the evolution of the modern corporation.

As Rumelt (1974) demonstrated in his study of corporate mergers and acquisitions in the 1950s and 1960s, an assessment of the outcomes associated with conglomerate mergers runs a continuum from successful to poor. Rumelt found that product related mergers generally produced satisfactory returns, whereas, product unrelated mergers produced poor returns. The research of Davis et al. (1994) on the deconglomeration movement of the 1980s provides evidence that much of the deconglomeration activity involves the divestiture of product unrelated divisions. This would be a corrective action taken in response to a growth strategy that failed to produce expected returns. The finance conception of control model is the logical extension of Taylor's scientific management principles from the shop floor to the corporate board room. The underlying social process explaining the ascendancy of the finance conception of corporate control is nothing more than the uninterrupted continuation of the historical rationalization process depicted by Weber (1978). And yes, ideas and power are important but only to the extent that they are successful in meeting the interests and needs of the social groupings affected. As Fligstein (1996) acknowledges "markets are political constructions," and successful politics in a democratic setting is embedded in the art of satisfying diverse interests. The primary competing interests in organizations are employees, managers, and the shareholder interests represented by the Board of Directors. It is the competing interests of managers and shareholders (represented by the Board of Directors) which have the greatest implications for evaluating corporate strategies.

The separation of ownership and control which characterizes the modern corporation creates an accountability gap between shareholders and managers of firms. Managers of large corporations have a measure of autonomy due to large organizational size. Large organization size is correlated with diffuse ownership which provides managers with the opportunity to pursue their own interests rather than the interests of the shareholders. The financial markets perspective posits that shareholders can hold managers accountable by demanding returns on their investments that are comparable with the returns accrued in similar organizations. Therefore, the principle-agent problem can be mitigated by shareholder demands for competitive returns (returns comparable to some market average) or they are likely to exercise their option to seek higher returns by supporting a merger with more profitable firms. In the case of mergers, managers of acquired firms are replaced by the management of the acquiring firm. Therefore, shareholder threat of merger is a credible threat that can be effectively employed to hold management accountable to shareholder interests. Shareholders can exercise the option of merger even when they are satisfied with managerial performance if they perceive that higher returns can be achieved through merger.

Banking research indicates that the shareholders of acquired firms benefit the most in the short-term from mergers because of the substantial premium paid them above the market value of their stock.[3] An evaluation of whether the premiums paid shareholders of the acquired bank are high or low depends on calculation of many factors. The returns provided shareholders of acquired banks must be based on an objective assessment of the potential long-term returns that can be earned by the acquiring holding company. The premium paid shareholders of the acquired bank is based on several factors. The objective of the acquiring holding company is to expand into a new market. By buying an established bank, the multi-bank holding company is acquiring an established customer base with its accumulated goodwill, as well as, trained staff, and plant and equipment. Also, if the acquired bank is not performing to expectations, additional returns can be accrued from improving the acquired bank's performance. Therefore, the returns on assets of subsidiaries of multi-bank holding companies should be higher than those of independent banks, especially in non-branch banking states, due to gains in efficiency provided by the acquiring holding company. This prediction follows from the hypothesis that economies of scale and scope can be achieved through the acquisition of relatively small, independent banks, and the hypothesis that multi-bank holding companies are more likely to acquire underperforming banks. Since returns on assets is a measure of profitability, increasing returns on assets signifies the potential for management to increase shareholder returns either through increased dividends or increased share value. A primary motive for the acquisition of banks by multi-bank holding companies is the potential to increase the return on assets of acquired banks which can be translated in higher, long-term profitability for the shareholders of the acquiring holding company. This is the principal rationale for the diffusion of the multi-bank holding company form which is driving the transformation in the structure of commercial banking.

One of the problems with evaluating the performance of firms is the lack of standard performance measures. Most studies of financial performance rely on indicators such as firm growth and earnings per common share of stock. However, better measures of financial performance are return on assets (an indicator of firm profitability) and return on equity (an indicator of shareholder returns). In addition to being the most common performance indicators used in the banking industry, their primary recommendation lies in their ability to facilitate inter-bank comparisons (Koch 1992:114-121). Return on assets is defined as the ratio of net income to total assets. Banks generate operating revenues from the interest earned on their assets which are the loans and investments they make. A bank's net income is calculated by subtracting net operating expenses from net revenues. When holding the level of assets constant, an increase in net income leads to an absolute increase in the return on assets ratio. Hence, return on assets is an indicator of a bank's profitability and its utilization of assets.

Another important gauge of bank performance is return on equity. Return on equity is defined as the ratio of net income to total shareholder equity. Shareholder equity is the total dollar value of outstanding capital stock and retained earnings. Return on equity is a better comparative measure of banks' ability to meet shareholder demands than earnings per common share or net income (Cole 1972:42). Return on equity relates profits to the average dollar value of equity, whereas, earnings per share relates dollar profits to the average number of outstanding shares of stock which is variable across firms. It is better to compare dollar profit to dollar investment than it is to compare dollar profit to the number of outstanding shares of common stock. Net income, in and of itself, is only a measure of profit and does not indicate the degree to which it is related to the dollar value of assets or to the dollar value of outstanding shareholder equity.

Return on equity is an important concept for measuring the ability of banks to meet shareholder demands and is a valid concept for making inter-bank comparisons.

Return on equity models are central components of the firm-as-portfolio model or finance conception of the firm (Copeland and Weston 1992). The capital structure of a bank can be characterized in a variety of ways. The ratio of shareholder equity to performing assets is used as a measure a bank's capitalization. A high capitalization ratio provides the bank a hedge against economic adversity. The ratio of equity to performing assets can be manipulated to improve shareholder returns by decreasing the level of equity in the bank. The gains achieved by decreasing equity in a bank are offset by an increase in risk. The equity multiplier is a measure designed to track banks' capital structure and to evaluate its risk factor. The equity multiplier is defined as the ratio of assets to shareholder equity and measures the extent to which a bank relies on equity and non-equity funds to finance assets. An equity multiplier of 10 indicates that a bank has $10 of assets for every $1 of equity. Banks with low returns on assets can produce a respectable return on equity by reducing the equity in the bank which equates with increasing the equity multiplier. The converse is that banks with low equity multipliers must have high returns on assets to produce comparable returns on equity. The mix of equity capital and leverage within a firm govern shareholder returns and capital risk.

The capital structure ratios are expected to have a significant impact on the financial performance banks (Cole 1972; Koch 1992:115-18).[4] There is a trade-off between the level of risk shareholders and managers are willing to accept. The lower the ratio of capital to assets the greater the potential return to shareholders, but at the same time, fewer assets need to go into default before the bank becomes insolvent. Therefore, it is an empirical question as to the appropriate mix of equity capital to assets. It is reasonable to expect banks with high returns on assets to have relatively low equity multipliers and relatively high capitalization ratios. On the other hand, it is possible for banks with high returns on equity to have above average equity multiplier ratios and average or below average capitalization ratios.[5]

Only in the past twenty years have the above measures of bank performance become widely adopted in commercial banking. In a 1971 survey of second-year students at Stonier Graduate School of Banking, sixty percent of the students stated that the primary goal of bank managers is to increase the dollar level of earning per common share. In the same survey, eighty-five percent of the students stated that their primary objective in terms of profits was to realize percentage growth in net income (Cole 1972:40). Other bank surveys in the 1960s and early 1970s found that most bankers at the time did not focus on return on assets or return on equity ratios. While they did concentrate on shareholder returns, they did not relate returns to shareholders investments. Relating firm returns to shareholder investments defines the recent finance revolution in American business. The volatile inflationary period of the late 1970s and 1980s firmly rooted the finance conception of control in the minds of American business. It is to be expected that bank holding companies have an advantage in attracting the most competent financial managers and this has propelled the bank holding company movement in commercial banking as bank shareholders seek to maximize the returns on their investments.

On a final note, not all banks have the same preference orderings. In addition to profit maximization, bankers may value the status, power, and prestige they hold in their communities. Organizational research has demonstrated that the desire for generalized rewards such as status and power can be as important as money for motivation of behavior (Homans 1974). Due to their role as trustees of monetary deposits and as sources of funds for borrowers, bankers are centrally positioned in the allocation of financial resources to businesses and individuals. The centrality of banking to economic activity is the source of bankers' power and status within their service markets (Koch 1992:878). The control over scarce and valued monetary resources in a community and the power and prestige it brings can be a powerful inducement for bank strategies that are designed to maintain autonomy and independence from the large multi-bank holding companies. From this it is to be expected that there may be many relatively profitable independent banks which desire to maintain the status quo—to not form a multi-bank holding company or to be acquired by one. One strategy for remaining independent is to form a one-bank holding company. However, for the one-bank holding company strategy to work, the managers must produce acceptable rates of returns to their shareholders.

DATA AND METHODS

Data

The source of the bank data is the Board of Governors of the Federal Reserve System. The Federal Reserve's *Bank Holding Company File* contains historical data on bank holding companies and their subsidiaries. The bank holding company file provides chartering and acquisition dates (day/month/year) for all bank holding company events which include application dates, approval/rejection dates, and divestiture dates. The bank financial data comes from the Federal Reserve Board's quarterly *Report of Income and Condition* which contains detailed financial information on all commercial banks in the United States. Due to availability and cost constraints, only data from the fourth quarter (end of year) editions for the years 1977-1988 are used in the study. This period is believed important since it covers a period which includes major legislative federal and state legislative action, and also, a great number bank holding company foundings. The source for state population and income data is the *Statistical Abstract of the United States* published annually by the Census Bureau.

I maintain that the diffusion of the bank holding company form is dependent on the incentives it provides bank shareholders and managers. One of the central hypotheses is that the legitimation of the bank holding company form is contingent on its ability to improve on the financial performance of acquired banks. The two dependent variables which are measures of financial performance are return on assets and return on equity. Both measures of financial performance are constructed from variables that have been transformed into constant 1991 dollars.

A central proposition of this study is that rational action is mediated by the prevailing institutional order. In this analysis of bank performance, institutions vary at two basic levels; 1) variation in the organization form of individual banks, and 2) variation in state branch banking laws. Therefore, it is to be expected that both return on assets and return on equity will vary by type of bank form and by type of state branch banking law. To account for the variation in financial performance across types of bank form, two separate analyses are performed, one for non-branch banking states and one for branch banking states. Non-branch banking states includes both limited branch banking states and unit branch banking states. The merging of limited branch and unit banking states is relevant because most unit branch banking states had changed their branch banking regulations by 1988 (see Table 4-1). The justification for performing separate analyses of bank performance is based on the assumption that banks operating in branch banking states are sufficiently diversified to weather the effects of recessions and economic crises, and therefore, have less incentive to adopt new bank forms. In addition to institutional effects, the financial performance of banks is affected by bank characteristics and various environmental factors. The explanatory variables are:

Institutional Variables:

"multi-bank holding companies"—a dummy variable with independent banks as the omitted category.

"one-bank holding companies"—a dummy variable with independent banks as the omitted category.

"subsidiaries"—a dummy variable for banks that are subsidiaries on multi-bank holding companies with independent banks as the omitted category.

"independent banks"—banks that are not part of a multi- or one-bank holding company structure.

"federal reserve member"—a dummy variable indicating member banks of the Federal Reserve with non-member banks the omitted category.

Capital Structure:

"capitalization"—ratio of equity capital to total assets in constant 1991 dollars.

"equity multiplier"—ratio of total assets to equity capital in constant 1991 dollars.

Bank Characteristics:

"bank age"—a banks age since founding in years.

"log assets"—the logarithm of total bank assets in constant 1991 dollars (an indicator of the first order effect of bank size for moderate sized banks).

"log assets squared"—the logarithm of total bank assets in constant 1991 dollars squared (an indicator of the second order effect of bank size for very large banks.

"# branch banks"—the number of branch banks.

Control Variables:

"interest rate"—interest rate is approximated by an annual average of three
   month treasury bills.
"% state pop.urb."—the percentage of a state's population that resides in a
   SMA.
"state per capita income"—a state's per capita income in constant 1987
   dollars.
"oil state"—banks operating in Texas, Oklahoma, and Louisiana.
"region"—1) northeast, 2) south, 3)midwest, 4) west.

The values for percentage of state population in urban areas and state
per capita income are 1980 census estimates for the years 1978-1984 and
1990 census estimates for the years 1985-1988.

Descriptive statistics and zero order correlations are presented in Tables
5-1 and 5-2 respectively. Because I am analyzing a pooled, time series cross-
section data set, the time changing explanatory variables are measured at
times t-1 and t. The lagged value is measured at time t-1 and a change
variable is created measured as the difference between t-1 and t. Both the
lagged and change variables are included in the descriptive statistics tables
for quantitative explanatory variables. This will be explained further in the
methods section.

Methods

To study the financial performance of banks, a regression analysis of a
pooled time-series, cross-section (TSCS) data set is performed. The data set
contains eleven cross-sections, 1978 through 1988. Only banks with values
on all dependent and independent variables for each of the years are included
in the data set. This represents a loss of information on banks that were
founded or failed during the period of analysis. However, the loss of
information is less than the information gained from investigating the
dynamics of bank financial performance over the observation period. The
quantitative explanatory variables are lagged one year since it is assumed
that bank managers set goals and make decisions based on information
gathered in the recent past.

Table 5-1. Descriptive Statistics: 1978-1988 Data.

	Mean	Std.Dev.	Min.	Max.
Return on Assets	0.95	0.92	-37.57	13.46
Return on Equity	10.22	22.32	-974.50	945.20
MBHC	0.08	0.27	0.00	1.00
Subsidiary	0.10	0.30	0.00	1.00
OBHC	0.26	0.44	0.00	1.00
Independent	0.55	0.50	0.00	1.00
Equity Multiplier	12.52	5.16	1.04	328.10
Capitalization	0.09	0.03	1.0E-3	0.96
log Assets (size)	10.77	1.07	7.07	16.17
# Branch Banks	1.92	6.65	0.00	321.00
Interest Rate	8.64	2.67	4.97	14.02
% St. Pop. Urb.	65.52	17.66	18.33	99.19
St. Inc/Cap.	13931.10	1866.40	9540.00	22083.00
Bank Age	68.27	30.25	9.10	183.30
Fed. Res. Mem.	0.37	0.48	0.00	1.00
Oil State	0.15	0.36	0.00	1.00
Region	2.40	0.80	1.00	4.00

Table 5-2. Zero-Order Correlations: 1978-1988 Data.

	(1)	(2)	(3)	(4)	(5)	(6)	(7)	(8)
1) ROA	---							
2) Lag ROA	.51	---						
3) Change ROA	.55	-.44	---					
4) ROE	.58	.27	.34	---				
5) Lag ROE	.31	.68	-.33	.19	---			
6) MBHC	-.01	.01	-.01	.01	.02	---		
7) Subsidiary	-.05	-.06	.01	-.01	-.01	-.10	---	
8) OBHC	-.06	-.04	-.02	-.03	-.02	-.18	-.20	---
9) Independent	.09	.07	.02	.03	.02	-.33	-.38	-.66
10) Lag Eq.Mult.	-.22	-.42	.18	-.04	-.34	.05	.09	.05
11) Change EM	-.33	-.02	-.32	-.14	-.03	.01	.01	.02
12) Lag Capital.	.23	.34	-.09	.02	.10	-.07	-.12	-.08
13) Change Cap.	.31	.03	.29	.19	-.01	-.01	-.02	-.02
14) Lag logAsset	-.04	-.02	-.02	.03	.05	.21	.19	-.01
15) Chng lnAss	.15	.10	.05	.13	.09	.02	.03	-.03
16) Lag lnAssSq	-.38	-.02	-.02	.03	.05	.22	.19	-.01
17) Chng lnAssSq	-.02	-.03	.01	-.01	-.03	.01	.03	-.01
18) Lag # Branch	-.02	-.03	.01	.01	.01	.13	.08	-.02
19) Chng # Bran	-.01	-.01	-.01	.01	.01	.04	.04	-.01
20) Lag Interest	.01	.09	-.08	-.01	.04	.02	.01	.04
21) Change Int.	.11	.07	.05	.07	.06	-.06	-.04	-.13
22) % St.Pop.Urb	-.02	-.02	.01	-.01	-.01	.02	.05	-.09
23) St. Inc/Cap	-.09	-.10	.01	-.04	-.05	.08	.08	.12
24) Bank Age	.06	.06	.01	.03	.03	.03	-.01	-.01
25) Branch St.	.01	-.01	.01	.01	.01	-.01	.01	-.09
26) Fed.Res.Mem	-.02	-.02	-.01	.01	-.01	.04	.09	-.05
27) Oil State	-.02	.02	-.04	-.02	-.01	.01	-.02	.02
28) Region	-.04	-.04	-.01	-.02	-.02	.02	-.01	.14

Table 5-2. (Continued)

	(9)	(10)	(11)	(12)	(13)	(14)	(15)	(16)
9) Independent	---							
10) Lag Eq.Mult.	-.12	---						
11) Change EM	-.03	-.28	---					
12) Lag Capital.	.19	-.58	.02	---				
13) Change Cap.	.04	.16	-.30	-.24	---			
14) Lag lnAss	-.22	.21	.01	-.32	.04	---		
15) Chng. lnAss	.01	-.06	.02	.10	-.34	.01	---	
16) Lag lnAssSq	-.23	.21	.01	-.31	.03	.99	.01	---
17) Chng lnAssSq	-.02	.01	.02	.04	-.04	.01	.48	.01
18) Lag # Branch	-.10	.11	-.01	-.13	-.01	.50	.06	.53
19) Chng # Bran	-.04	.02	.01	-.02	-.04	.13	.27	.14
20) Lag Interest	-.05	-.05	.01	.04	-.02	-.01	.14	-.01
21) Change Int.	.18	.01	-.02	-.02	.04	-.03	-.15	-.03
22) % St.Pop.Urb	.03	.06	.01	-.05	-.02	.20	.07	.20
23) St. Inc/Cap	-.21	.07	.01	-.06	-.01	.12	.05	.12
24) Bank Age	-.01	-.06	-.02	.04	.06	.10	-.09	.10
25) Branch St.	.08	.03	-.01	.01	-.01	.16	.09	.17
26) Fed.Res.Mem	-.04	.07	.01	-.08	-.01	.28	-.01	.28
27) Oil State	-.01	.01	.05	.01	-.03	.01	.01	-.01
28) Region	-.14	.01	-.01	.01	.01	-.23	-.07	-.22

(cont.)	(17)	(18)	(19)	(20)	(21)	(22)	(23)	(24)
17) Chng lnAssSq	---							
18) Lag # Branch	.04	---						
19) Chng # Bran	.35	.21	---					
20) Lag Interest	.01	.01	.01	---				
21) Change Int.	-.02	-.02	-.01	-.47	---			
22) % St.Pop.Urb	.03	.08	.04	-.01	-.01	---		
23) St. Inc/Cap	.03	.05	.03	-.12	-.12	.55	---	
24) Bank Age	-.04	.08	.01	.00	.00	-.10	-.02	---
25) Branch St.	.03	.24	.06	.00	.00	.13	.19	-.06
26) Fed.Res.Mem	.01	.09	.03	.00	.00	.09	.06	.15
27) Oil State	-.01	-.08	-.02	.00	.00	.19	-.10	-.12
28) Region	-.02	-.16	-.05	.00	.00	.24	.11	-.11

(cont.)	(25)	(26)	(27)	(28)
25) Branch St.	---			
26) Fed.Res.Mem	.06	---		
27) Oil State	-.14	.05	---	
28) Region	-.07	-.15	-.09	---

N = 151152

To justify the use of the TSCS, I first analyzed each of the eleven cross-sections by ordinary least squares (OLS). While the estimates vary somewhat over the cross-sections, the overall pattern suggests sufficient structural stability to justify TSCS. The incorporation of both cross-sectional and temporal information provided by panel designs enhances the modeling of social dynamics. But there is a price to pay since the complex data structure of TSCS introduces particular statistical concerns.

The estimation of TSCS data with ordinary least squares (OLS) estimators is often problematic.[6] OLS estimators are premised on the assumption that the effects of excluded explanatory variables attributed to the error term are independently and normally distributed with zero mean and constant variance, $e_{it} \sim IN(0,\sigma)$. Violation of these assumptions results in biased and inefficient OLS estimates. When estimating models with TSCS data sets, heteroscedasticity and autocorrelation are of particular concern. Since observations are not temporally independent within cases, autocorrelated disturbances are very likely. Also, autocorrelation of the disturbances is "inherent" with the inclusion of lagged dependent variables. This is so because that part of the estimated dependent variable, $y(t)$, which is attributable to omitted explanatory variables is automatically transferred from one period to the next by the lagged dependent variable $y(t-1)$. Tests for the presence of autocorrelation were performed, and the tests indicated autocorrelated disturbances within cases over the observation period, but the effects on the estimates were negligible.

Also, a TSCS data structure increases the likelihood of heteroscedasticity which violates the constant variance assumption of OLS. There are two sources of heteroscedasticity since nonconstant variance can arise spatially (across cases within cross-sections) and temporally (within cases over time). Therefore, the error term may consist of unmodeled case specific, cross-section effects (variation across cases within cross-sections), time specific effects (variation within cases over time), or a combination of both. In the bank financial performance analysis, case specific effects are possible consequences of unmodeled variation in banks' customer base and/or variation in the competency of bank management. It is likely that both of these unmodeled effects are related to variation in banks' size. Larger banks are more likely to have a customer base which includes the dominant and more established businesses in the community such as utilities, government, large businesses and community organizations, whereas, the customer base of relatively smaller banks is comprised primarily of smaller and more variable accounts. While bank size is controlled in the analysis, it is likely that unmodeled variation in customer base and managerial competency will contribute to heteroscedastic disturbances. These case specific effects are perceived as relatively stable over the observation period. State branch banking laws is another source of nonconstant variance between banks within cross-sections and is resolved by separating the financial performance analysis into two parts—one for banks operating in branch banking states and the other for banks operating in non-branch banking states.

Time specific effects arising from changing economic conditions could be a cause of non-constant variance within specific cases over the observation period. While within case variation over time is plausible due to the number of regional economic crises that occurred over the observation period, it is likely to present a less serious problem than across case variation because of the few time periods (11) in relation to the number of cross-section observations (1041 and 9465). Since model specification controls for many of the most obvious sources of variation, the unmodeled effects case specific and temporal effects are modeled as random rather than as fixed effects. The appropriate method for modeling random case specific and temporal effects is an error components model (Fuller and Battese 1974; Johnston 1984:400-06; Greene 1990:485-495).

The estimation equation for the financial performance analyses takes the form

$$y_{it} = b_0 + b_n X_{itn} + u_{it}$$

where i is the number of cases in each cross-section, n is the number of independent variables, and t is the number of time periods (the number of cross-sections). The error structure of u is comprised of three components such that

$$u_{it} = m_i + v_t + e_{it},$$

where m_i are individual case effects, v_t are the time specific effects, and e_{it} are the normal, random error components. Various diagnostic tests suggest that both case specific and time specific effects are present, as well as, autocorrelated disturbances. The financial performance models were estimated with an error components model (SAS' Fuller-Batiste TSCS model) which is a generalized least squares estimator and controls for both case and time specific effects.[7]

The dependent variables in this chapter are the financial performance variables, return on assets and return on equity. Since this is a dynamic analysis, the coefficients of the explanatory variables are estimating the degree of change in the dependent variables over time. Since an instantaneous rate of change is unobservable and cannot be estimated, the strategy is to first estimate the integral form of bank financial performance using generalized least squares and then to derive the parameters of the dynamic, differential equation model from the parameters of the integral form.[8] The transformed coefficient estimates represent the underlying dynamic effects of the differential equation model.

The adjustment parameter ranges in value from 0 to 1, and it is interpreted as the degree of stability in the initial value of the dependent variable in each of the yearly time intervals over the eleven year observation period. An adjustment parameter approaching 0 indicates a stable value of the dependent variable with little adjustment from the initial value. An adjustment parameter approaching 1 indicates that there is significant movement from the initial value of the dependent variable in each yearly interval over the observation period. An adjustment parameter approaching 0 indicates stability in the initial value of the financial performance variable in each of the yearly intervals over the eleven year observation period. On the other hand, an adjustment parameter approaching 1 indicates that significant change in the initial value of the financial performance variable is occurring in each of the time intervals. Since the values of the financial performance variables are decreasing over the observation period, movement from the initial value of financial performance variable indicates a decrease in the financial performance. A low value for the adjustment parameter indicates relatively stable financial performance over the observation period which is an indicator of strong performance in this particular scenario. In contrast, a high value of the adjustment parameter indicates unstable or rapid decreases in financial performance over the observation period. I expect the adjustment parameters' for banks operating in branch banking states to be closer to zero than the adjustment parameter for banks operating in non-branch banking states. This would indicate greater stability in financial performance. The estimated coefficients for the effects of the explanatory variables are simply interpreted as an increase or decrease in the long-term level of financial performance.

FINDINGS

A summary of aggregate bank financial performance is presented in Table 5-3. The averages are calculated by type of bank form and by type of branch banking law. The financial performance of banks in branch banking states is much more stable over the observation than is the financial performance of banks in non-branch banking states as evidenced by the substantially lower variances. This is consistent with the argument that banks in branch banking states are able to better diversify their asset base to counter the cyclic nature of local economies. While returns were initially higher in non-branch banking states, the decrease in returns for banks in non-branch banking states was severe over the observation period, whereas, the change returns was marginal for banks in branch banking states. This supports the hypothesis that during periods of volatile economic conditions the financial performance of banks in branch banking states should be more stable and on average higher than the financial performance of banks in non-branch banking states. On a final note, the variances in returns for one-bank holding companies is significantly greater than the variance of other bank forms in both branch and non-branch banking states.

The analysis of return on assets (ROA) in presented in Table 5-4, and the analysis of return on equity (ROE) is presented in Table 5-5. The estimates reported in the tables have been transformed and represent estimates of the differential equation model. The models provide estimates of two distinct phenomena: 1) the average rate of adjustment in financial performance in each of the yearly intervals over the observation period; and 2) the effect of the explanatory variables on the final level of financial performance at the end of the observation period, 1988.

The rate of adjustment for return on assets is .10 in branch banking states and .11 in non-branch banking states. This indicates that a slow adjustment process is occurring in both types of branch banking regimes. The process of adjustment in each period appears to be incremental, and therefore, relatively stable since the effects of the higher initial level of return

Table 5-3. Mean Return on Assets and Mean Return on Equity by Type
of State Branch Banking Law and Type of Bank Form.*

A. Branch Banking States:

	Return on Assets				Return on Equity			
Year:	MBHC	SUBS	OBHC	INDEP	MBHC	SUBS	OBHC	INDEP
1978	.86	.86	.94	.91	12.3	11.9	12.9	0.8
1979	.89	.94	.98	1.06	12.4	12.5	13.6	12.0
1980	.89	1.02	1.02	1.08	12.1	12.7	12.8	11.7
1981	.90	1.07	.89	1.06	11.6	12.4	11.1	11.3
1982	.86	.95	.72	.98	10.7	11.7	8.2	10.0
1983	.85	.91	.58	1.00	11.3	11.6	2.7	10.6
1984	.83	.95	.72	1.03	11.2	12.5	11.1	11.2
1985	.82	.99	.79	1.08	12.0	12.8	9.6	10.3
1986	.83	.86	.80	.95	11.4	10.9	10.0	8.6
1987	.87	.92	.85	.97	10.8	12.2	10.0	10.0
1988	.93	.94	.88	1.05	11.2	12.2	9.9	10.9
Mean	.87	.95	.83	1.02	11.5	12.1	10.2	10.7
Var.	.01	.04	.89	.03	3.4	3.2	88.0	8.9

N = 1041

****

B. Non-Branch Banking States:

	Return on Assets				Return on Equity			
Year:	MBHC	SUBS	OBHC	INDEP	MBHC	SUBS	OBHC	INDEP
1978	1.06	.96	1.05	1.02	13.8	13.0	13.5	12.0
1979	1.16	1.07	1.23	1.16	15.1	14.3	15.6	13.3
1980	1.24	1.13	1.34	1.20	15.6	14.6	16.2	13.2
1981	1.21	1.08	1.30	1.16	15.1	13.9	15.5	12.4
1982	1.19	.99	1.19	1.08	14.7	12.8	13.7	11.2
1983	1.08	.86	1.01	1.03	13.0	11.1	11.4	10.2
1984	.95	.82	.82	.94	11.0	10.7	8.4	9.0
1985	.88	.67	.74	.90	9.9	7.4	7.5	8.2
1986	.76	.53	.58	.75	8.1	4.2	3.8	6.2
1987	.74	.68	.65	.73	7.7	6.3	5.2	5.4
1988	.77	.66	.72	.76	9.1	8.7	6.8	6.7
Mean	1.00	.86	.97	.98	12.1	10.6	10.7	9.8
Var.	.37	.40	.76	.30	91.1	124.7	203.2	82.7

N = 9465

* -- Only banks with full information (1978-1988) included.

Table 5-4. Return on Assets -- Commercial Bank Performance, 1988. Pooled Cross-Section, Time Series: Partial Adjustment Models.

Variables:	Branch Banking States	Non-Branch Banking States
Rate of Adjustment	0.097	0.111
Institutions		
Multi-Bank Holding Co.	-0.010*	0.026**
Subsidiaries	-0.002	0.018**
One-Bank Holding Co.	-0.006*	0.018**
Federal Reserve Member	0.001**	-2.0E-3*
Characteristics		
Capitalization	1.102**	5.060**
Equity Multiplier	-0.009**	-0.004**
Log Assets	0.107**	0.520**
Log Assets Squared	-0.029**	-0.146**
# Branch Banks	-0.001**	-0.003**
Bank Age	1.4E-4**	8.5E-5**
Controls		
Interest Rate	0.002	0.008**
% State Pop. Urban	-1.1E-4**	-0.001**
State Per Capita Income	1.3E-6**	2.2E-6**
Region	-0.005**	-9.0E-4
Oil State	---	-2.9E-4
Constant	0.148	0.157**
Number of Cross-Sections	1041	9465
Number of Panels	11	11

** - $p < .01$; * - $p < .05$

Table 5-5. Return on Equity -- Commercial Bank Performance,
1978-1988. Pooled Cross-Section, Time Series: Partial
Adjustment Models.

Variables:	Branch Banking States	Non-Branch Banking States
Rate of Adjustment	0.157	0.974
Institutions		
Multi-Bank Holding Co.	0.129	0.397
Subsidiaries	0.156*	0.586**
One-Bank Holding Co.	0.105	0.092
Federal Reserve Member	-0.001	0.181**
Characteristics		
Return on Assets (t-1)	3.399**	15.254**
Capitalization	-13.206**	21.936**
Equity Multiplier	-0.004	0.347**
Log Assets	2.301**	11.456**
Log Assets Squared	-0.569**	-2.867**
# Branch Banks	-0.016**	-0.068**
Bank Age	3.8E-4	-5.5E-4**
Controls		
Interest Rate	0.008	0.014**
% State Pop. Urban	-0.001	-0.006**
State Per Capita Income	-1.8E-5	2.0E-4**
Region	0.009	0.054**
Oil State	---	-1.094**
Constant	-0.784	-19.875**
Number of Cross-Sections	1041	9465
Number of Panels	11	11

** - $p < .01$; * - $p < .05$

on assets persists to great extent in each of the yearly intervals over the observation period. Because return on assets is less variable in branch banking states than in non-branch banking, the slightly lower coefficient of adjustment in branch banking states is expected.

The rate of adjustment parameter in the return on equity models are presented in Table 5-5. The rate of adjustment for return on equity in branch banking states is .16 signifying a relatively slow and stable process of change in the yearly intervals over the observation period. However, the rate of adjustment on return on equity in non-branch banking states is .97 which indicates a very rapid decrease in each of the yearly intervals over the eleven year observation period. This finding signifies that on average banks in non-branch banking states were experiencing significant decreases in their return on equity in the 1980s, while banks in branch banking were experiencing relative stability. These results clearly support the hypothesis that branch banking laws present a more favorable climate for banking in periods of economic uncertainty.

The findings related to the effects of bank form on financial performance across banking regimes is quite interesting. Keep in mind that the estimated effects for each of the bank forms reported in the tables is in direct comparison to independent banks which is the excluded category for each of the bank form dummy variables. This comparison is deemed significant because the purpose of this study is to investigate the effect of the transition from independent bank to bank holding company on financial performance. The effect of bank form on return on assets is reported first, then the effect of bank form on return on equity is presented.

All the bank form variables, the institutional variables, have a statistically significant effect on return on assets in non-branch banking states. Lead banks of multi-bank holding companies, lead banks of one-bank holding companies, and subsidiaries of multi-bank holding companies have an expected long-term level of return on assets that is higher than the return on assets for independent banks. The key finding here is that return on assets for subsidiaries of multi-bank holding companies are higher than the return on assets for independent banks. A different picture emerges from the findings in branch banking states. In branch banking states, the variables having a statistically significant effect on return on assets are multi-bank and one-bank holding companies. In both cases, the expected long-term level of return on equity is lower than it is for independent banks. Being a subsidiary of multi-bank holding company in a branch banking state does not have a statistically significant effect on the long-term level of return on assets in comparison to independent banks.

These return on assets findings indicate that the multi-bank holding companies do have superior performance to independent banks in terms of return on assets in non-branch banking states. The positive effect of the one-bank holding company on return on assets, once again, suggests that the lead banks of one-bank holding companies have strong financial performance. This is another indication that one of the motives for forming one-bank holding companies is to create a shield against acquisition attempts. In branch banking states, the negative effects of the holding company form supports the contention that scale and scope economies are attained at relatively modest bank size, and therefore, there are no advantages to the holding company form in improving bank performance in terms of return on assets.

The effects of bank form on return on equity are consistent across branch banking regimes. Being a subsidiary of a multi-bank holding company has the only statistically significant effect on the long-term level of return on equity. In both branch and non-branch banking states, subsidiaries on multi-bank holding companies have a higher long-term level of return on equity than independent banks. Since the return on equity of multi-bank holding companies can be translated into higher returns for the parent multi-bank holding company, this is a very significant finding. While the coefficients for the lead banks of multi-bank and one-bank holding are positive, they are not statistically significant. In conclusion, the return on equity findings provide clear evidence that the bank holding company form performs adequately in comparison to independent banks, especially regarding the positive and statistically significant effects for subsidiaries of multi-bank holding companies.

The effects of capital structure on the long-term return on assets level is as predicted. A more conservative capital structure, a high ratio of equity to assets and a low ratio of assets to equity, leads to a higher long-term level of return on assets in both branch and non-branch banking states. These findings are statistically significant. As previously explained, a conservative capital structure must generate high returns on assets in order to yield satisfactory shareholder returns. In contrast, banks with a low return on assets ratio must either yield low shareholder returns or alter the capital structure by reducing the ratio of equity to assets, and thereby, increase risk.

When the effects of capital structure on long-term return on equity is examined an interesting picture emerges. In branch banking states, the effect of capitalization on return on equity is negative and statistically significant. The equity multiplier coefficient is not statistically significant. In contrast, the effects of both capitalization and equity multiplier in non-branch banking states are positive and statistically significant. A high equity multiplier by definition should be associated with a higher return on equity, but it also represents greater risk.

The first order effect of bank size, measured in terms of assets, are positive and statistically significant for both return on assets and return on equity in branch and non-branch banking states. The second order effect of bank size which measures the effects of very large banks are negative and statistically significant for both return on assets and return on equity in both branch and non-branch banking states. The effects for number of branch banks is also negative and statistically significant for both return on assets and return on equity in branch and non-branch banking states. These findings on the effects of bank size strongly suggest that economies are associated with moderate bank size and that diseconomies are realized for very large banks. Bank age has a positive, statistically significant effect on the long-term level of return on assets in both branch and non-branch banking states. The effect of bank age on return to equity is not statistically significant in branch banking states, and has a negative, statistically significant effect on return on equity in non-branch banking states.

As expected, lagged (previous year) return on assets has a positive and statistically significant effect on the long-term level of return on equity in both branch and non-branch banking states. Contrary to expectations, the percentage of a state's population living in urban areas has a negative effect on both return on assets and return on equity. A state's per capita income has a positive effect on both return on assets and return on equity as expected. The effects of being a Federal Reserve member bank on financial performance is inconsistent and difficult to interpret. As expected, oil state has a negative effect on financial performance.

DISCUSSION AND SUMMARY

It is important to note that the conclusions relating to bank holding companies are based on data for the lead banks of the holding companies and not on data for the parent holding company. Since I am interested in the differential performance of individual commercial banks, this data limitation does not affect my conclusions. The findings clearly indicate that lead banks and subsidiaries of multi-bank holding companies generate higher returns on equity than do independent banks regardless of type of state branch banking law. This holds true for the lead banks of one-bank holding companies as well. However, the picture is mixed when analyzing the effects of bank holding companies on return on assets. The effect of being the lead bank of a multi-bank company on return on assets is negative in branch banking states and positive in non-branch banking states. These results make sense in that banks in branch banking states have had the opportunity to expand into desired markets which has enabled them to realize scale and scope economies and to optimize on marginal unit costs. On the other hand, banks in non-branch banking states have been constrained in their ability to realize scale and scope economies. Therefore, it makes sense to conclude that the bank holding company form is a good adaptation to conditions in non-branch banking environments.

The most significant financial performance findings in relation to this study are the findings regarding subsidiaries of multi-bank holding companies. In Chapter 4, the analysis of bank acquisitions indicated that multi-bank companies tend to acquire banks with below average return on assets and return on equity. Now it is shown that subsidiaries of multi-bank holding companies have statistically significant higher return on assets in comparison to independent banks in non-branch banking states. Also, subsidiaries of multi-bank holding companies have a higher return on equity in both branch and non-branch banking states compared to independent banks. The conclusion drawn from these findings is that multi-bank holding companies acquire relatively under-performing independent banks and through management and capital restructuring are able to improve the financial performance of acquired banks. This is accomplished without diminishing the financial performance of lead banks of multi-bank holding companies in non-branch banking states. Therefore, it is reasonable to conclude that the multi-bank holding company growth strategy is successful for both the holding company and the acquired banks. Since the observation period is one of considerable economic stress and uncertainty in the financial services industry, this is a very significant finding and can be interpreted as a valid explanation for the diffusion of the multi-bank holding company form.

The contrasts in the financial performance of bank forms across branch banking regimes supports the hypothesis that external institutional arrangements can, and do in some instances, affect firm-level economic outcomes. Therefore, it is important to consider the possible implications of the interaction between rational action by firms and field-level governing institutions, e.g. laws and regulations. In branch banking states, banking markets are more developed in terms of statewide competition than are the historically protected local or regional markets in non-branch banking states. Hence, the positive benefits accruing the market extension acquisition strategies of multi-bank holding companies in non-branch banking states. This provides an explanation for why the lead banks of bank holding companies in branch banking states are not performing as well as bank holding companies in non-branch banking states. It is also instructive to note the negative effect of very large size on financial performance. The negative effect of very large size on financial performance will possibly influence the extent of the effect of regional and national banking networks on the long-term structure of commercial banking in the United States.

In many instances the formation of one-bank holding companies is designed as a strategy by profitable independent banks to resist takeover attempts (Eccles 1982). Therefore, it is interesting to note the remarkable parallels between the effects of banks forming one-bank holding companies and the lead banks of multi-bank holding companies on financial performance across state branch banking laws. The findings indicate that the one-bank holding company is a successful strategy for maintaining independence at least in non-branch banking states. The similarities in the performance of lead banks of multi-bank holding companies and one-bank holding companies suggest that on average the one-bank holding companies are positioned to become a multi-bank holding company if the desire arises. The fate of the one-bank holding company will be interesting to follow and will determine to a great extent whether a hybrid version of independent bank will remain a viable force in the future of commercial banking.

The significant effects of capital structure on bank performance provides further evidence of the saliency of the finance conception of control in

American business. My analysis covers a dark period in American banking when many commentators were predicting a collapse in commercial banking similar to the collapse of the savings and loan industry. Anything but has occurred in commercial banking. Commercial banking has rebounded in the 1990s and is currently one of the most outstanding performers in the American economy (Kaufman and Mote 1994). Banks have been able to achieve this remarkable turnaround by restructuring their equity, liability, and asset bases through holding company founding and bank acquisitions.

Bank liabilities traditionally have been in the form of deposits but borrowed funds are replacing deposits because of declines in deposits attributable to increased competition in financial markets. Bank earnings have traditionally been based on assets composed of loans and federal government securities, but are increasingly taking the form of fees earned on off-balance sheet services in the form of services rendered in the securitization of loan portfolios such as home mortgages and automobile loans (Kaufman and Mote 1994; Personal Interviews[9]). This is an example of how finance marketing is playing an ever greater role in the world of everyday commercial banking. Banks with finance expertise are able to maximize their capital structure to maximize returns to shareholders with variable asset performance and at the same time manage risk. The final assessment of the success of the finance market approach has yet to be determined, but without a doubt is flexing its muscle in the world of commercial banking.

In conclusion, there is little doubt that in non-branch banking states the bank holding company movement is an adaptive strategy which has diffused because of the very real potential for short-term financial gains for acquired banks and long-term gains for multi-bank holding companies. The picture is not as clear in branch banking states. These conclusions are only tentative since the transformation is continuing. The study needs to be extended to tract the mergers between bank holding companies as nationwide banking systems are being built. Of particular interest will be the actions of one-bank holding companies. Will they be a force for maintaining the long tradition in this country of locally controlled independent banks or will they choose to become regional and national multi-bank holding companies?

NOTES

1. The theory of profit maximization can be found in any standard introductory microeconomic text such as Frank's (1991) *Microeconomics and Behavior*. The first order condition for a maximum is given by $dP/dx = dp(x)/dx - dTC(x)/dx = p - MC(x) = 0$, where P is profit, x is level of output, p is price of output, TC is total cost, and MC is marginal cost. The second order condition for a maximum is $d^2P/dx^2 = -dMC(x)/dx < 0$.

2. The formal representation of the constrained choice model is the same as the partial adjustment model. For a theoretical introduction to the partial adjustment model refer to *Social Dynamics* by Tuma and Hannan (1984:332-341) and *Basic Econometrics* by Gujarati (1995:599-601).

3. The premiums paid shareholders of acquired firms above the market value of their stock is payment for the accumulated goodwill of the acquired firm. Goodwill is the recognition of the value of an established customer base.

4. The inclusion of the equity multiplier and the capitalization variables is to simply control for factors deemed significant to the financial performance of banks (see footnote 4 for the mechanics of the equity model). The issue of capital structure on bank performance is much more complex than outlined here. Much recent attention as been focused on the issuance of debt as a replacement for equity capital due to tax advantages, and also on the possibility that there may be an optimal capital structure that contains both debt and equity (see Copeland and Weston 1992:497-536). While the relationship between debt and taxes codes may be particularly relevant in explaining merger and acquisition behavior, I am unable to explore this relationship due to lack of data on the equity/debt structure of independent banks and bank holding companies.

5. The specification of the equity model is:

$$ROE = ROA + EM + R,$$

where ROE (return on equity) is the ratio of net income to total equity, ROA (return on assets) is the ratio of net income to total assets, EM (equity multiplier) is the ratio of total assets to total equity, and R (risk factor) is the ratio of total equity to total assets. Note that the risk factor is the inverse of the equity multiplier.

Consider two competing banks with $100 million in assets and earning one percent on assets (Koch 1992:117-118). The first bank is financed with $95 million in liabilities (deposits and borrowed funds) and $5 million in equity. The second bank is financed with $90 million in liabilities and $10 million in equity. The equity multiplier for the first bank is 20 and the equity multiplier for the second bank is 10. The return on equity for the first bank is 20 percent (20 times .01) and the return on equity for the second bank is 10 percent (10 times .01). The return to shareholders of the first bank are twice those of the second bank. However, if the earnings of the two banks are negative then the shareholders of the first bank experience a loss that is twice as great as the loss to the shareholders of the second bank. Therefore, the equity multiplier represents risk as well as profitability.

The risk factor (the ratio of total equity to total assets) reflects the amount of assets that can go into default before a bank becomes insolvent. The risk factor is 5 percent for the first bank and 10 percent for the second bank. The two banks have identical asset positions, but the second bank is in a less risky position since twice the amount of its assets can default before it becomes insolvent compared with the first bank. The equity model provides an explanation of how bank holding companies have served to maximize shareholder wealth without necessarily increasing the efficiency of the banks' utilization of assets.

6. This discussion of pooled time-series, cross-section estimators is drawn from Greene (1990:461-498), Tuma and Hannan (1984:430-47), and Johnston (984:396-407).

7. A variety of models were estimated, fixed effects, random effects, ARIMA maximum likelihood (SAS AUTOREG), and the Da Silva cross-effects moving average (SAS TSCS). The results generated by these models are very similar to those presented in this paper..

8. In Appendix 3, I discuss the transformations of the coefficients of the integral model and derive the logic and interpretation of the underlying dynamic differential equation models.

9. The securitization of loans is a recent development whereby the loan departments of commercial bankers and other financial institutions originate loans—mortgage, real estate, automobile, etc.—and then sell the loans at a discount on the secondary securities market. The loans are packaged in $100 million dollar bundles by type, risk, and amortization. Banks then service the loans for a fee, but do not carry the risk of default, the secondary market carries the risk.

CHAPTER 6

Legitimation of the Multi-Bank Holding Company Form and Change in State Branch Banking Laws

In this chapter, processes related to the legitimation of the multi-bank holding company form and change in branch banking laws are explored. With these analyses, an attempt is made to specify the mechanisms which link the actions of individual banks to broad changes in the structure and governing institutions of commercial banking. In the early 1950s, there existed the belief that the holding company form would be banned by Congressional legislation. The Bank Holding Company Act of 1956, while not banning bank holding companies, was drafted with the stated intention of diminishing the viability holding companies within commercial banking. The legitimacy of the bank holding company at this point in time was low to non-existent. In addition, two thirds of the states had restrictions on branch banking within their states which meant that the legitimacy of unconstrained, statewide branch banking was low. The question addressed in this chapter is how a form (multi-bank holding company) and practice (statewide branch banking) becomes legitimated?

One way of evaluating the legitimacy of social behavior is to determine the extent to which particular actions are "taken-for-granted" under the circumstances (Meyer and Rowan 1977). But how do innovative behaviors become legitimated? Institutional theory predicts that those behaviors which prove successful in producing desired outcomes will diffuse and result in institutional change as they become "taken-for-granted" (Meyer and Rowan 1977; Friedman and Hechter 1988:203-04; Fligstein 1990; Nee and Lian

1994). The legitimation of innovative forms and practices in this scenario is premised on a simple aggregation mechanism which is based on the extent to which innovative practices diffuse throughout the social group. Thus, the legitimation of the multi-bank holding company form is determined by the correlation between growth, financial performance, and the preferences of bank managers and shareholders. A positive correlation among these elements provides a signal within the banking industry, that positive gains can be realized through the adoption of the multi-bank holding company form. The diffusion of the multi-bank holding company form can be seen as a memetic process that occurs through imitation and learning as banks observe and attempt to replicate the relatively more successful performance of multi-bank holding companies. The increasing number of banks controlled by multi-bank holding companies translates into pressure on state and federal authorities to liberalize branch banking laws. Change in branch banking laws represents the formal acceptance of the multi-bank holding company form as a legitimate means for achieving bank growth. In this scenario, legitimation can be interpreted as a selection process, whereby, the banking industry through capital markets select for survival those banks which produce satisfactory returns to investors in comparison to some average level of returns on other investment opportunities (Alchian 1950; Frank 1991:331).

However, it can be argued that a more complex process is driving the dynamics of change in the structure and institutions of commercial banking. Rather than a simple selection aggregation mechanism premised on the existence of homogeneous preferences for returns on investments, a more complex aggregation process may be warranted which takes into account heterogeneous preferences. As previously stated, over five thousand one-bank holding companies have been founded, and the evidence suggests the adoption of the one-bank holding company form is in many instances a defensive strategy on the part of independent banks desiring to retain their autonomy. This is consistent with the premise that generalized rewards other than monetary rewards such as status, power, and prestige are highly valued and serve as strong motivations for human behavior (Homans 1974). If this is the case, then it follows that there are conflicting views concerning the appropriate organizing form of banks. This parallels the historical picture of banking presented in Chapter 2. One segment of the banking industry supports a centralized, national banking system while another segment desires a decentralized, localized banking system. If this interpretation of the banking industry is correct, then it is plausible that a collective action model may be appropriate for explaining the changing structure and institutions of commercial banking. A collective action model focuses on the political mobilization process which translates individual interests into organized political power. Collective action theory explains the institutionalization process in terms of the relative bargaining power of competing interests within social groupings. Some collective interests within the group have power over others in the rule setting process. The collective action model is offered as an alternative explanation for the legitimation of the multi-bank holding company form through changes in branch banking laws. Before applying the collective action model to commercial banking, an explanation based on a selection model derived from organizational ecology is presented.

According to organizational ecology, organizational vital rates, i.e. organizational founding and mortality rates, are functions of legitimation and competition (Hannan and Freeman 1977, 1989; Hannan and Carroll 1992). But legitimation and competition are unobservable variables. Therefore, observable proxy variables have to be chosen to actually estimate the effects of legitimation and competition on organizational vital rates. Hannan and Freeman (1977, 1989) maintain that the density of organizational forms within an organizational field over time can be utilized as an appropriate approximation of legitimation and competition effects on organizational vital rates. In other words, organizational founding and mortality rates are density dependent. In the early history of an organizational form, legitimation effects are important in determining organizational vital rates. But once an organizational form proves successful within the resource environment comprising the organizational field, the effects of competition begin to dominate the effects of legitimation on organizational founding rates. The historical evolution of an organizational form within an organizational field is characterized by a non-monotonic function of density dependence. The founding rate of a new organizational form increases in the initial stages of its history due to increasing legitimacy, but over time founding rate continue to increase but at a decreasing rate due to the effects of increasing competition for limited resources. When the density of organizational forms within an organizational field approaches the carrying capacity of the resource environment to sustain the existing population of organizations, the founding rate of new organizations begins to decline.

Organizational fields select for survival those organizational forms which prove capable of sustaining some minimum level of resources. The organizational forms that survive the selection process are those forms that provide the best fit with the organizational resource environment. This selection process determines the variety of organizational forms that populate an organizational field. Selection and adaptation are flip-sides of the same coin. Selection operates at the population level of the organizational field, and adaptation operates at the level of the individual organization. Organizations attempt to adapt to changing environmental conditions such as increasing competition or changing technologies. The success of organizational adaptations is ultimately evaluated by population level selection processes. Those organizational forms and practices that prove successful in generating the level of resources needed for survival thrive while unsuccessful organizations cease to exist.

To apply the propositions of organization ecology to commercial banking, an evaluation of the resource boundaries of the organizational field is important. The historical function of commercial banking is to accept demand and time deposits and to earn revenues by making short-term commercial loans. The National Bank Acts of 1933 and 1935 provided commercial banks with a monopoly on demand deposits and prohibited them from paying interest on demand deposits. The net effect of these regulations was to provide commercial banks with a monopoly on an inexpensive source of funds with which to make loans and earn profits. In addition to these advantages, branch banking restrictions provided barriers to entry into commercial banking markets. In the early 1950s there were approximately 14,000 commercial banks. As previously noted, the benefits of sheltered markets in commercial banking began to be eroded in the booming economy of the 1950s and 1960s due to below market level interest rate ceilings on commercial bank deposits. Interest rate competition initiated by other sectors of the financial services industry cut into the share of loanable funds controlled by commercial banks (see Tables 2-1 and 2-2, p. 8). The increased competition in the market for loanable funds altered the incentive structure imposed by the regulatory environment of commercial banking. This set in motion the search for growth strategies to offset the loss of market share in loanable funds. Keep in mind, banks earn profits on the revenues generated from loans which means that a loss of loanable funds translates into a loss of revenues and profits. In essence, the resource environment of commercial banking was shrinking in by the late 1950s.

Banking at this time was a fully mature industry with all market niches served by existing banks. The most obvious way to achieve growth was through the acquisition of other banks. However, substantial obstacles stood in the path of banks acquiring other banks in the form of federal and state bank regulatory agencies. as well as, federal anti-trust law. Another important constraint on banks simply acquiring other banks was public opinion. Since banks are entrusted with the monetary assets of others, people like to know their bankers personally. The public's attitude in favor of conducting their banking business with locally controlled banks justified the use of the holding company form to acquire banks. Subsidiaries of multi-bank holding companies can keep their own identity and local officers which shields from public view the fact that the bank was no longer locally controlled. Therefore, before banks could be acquired on a large scale, their existed the need to legitimate the acquisition of locally controlled independent banks by multi-bank holding companies.

The resource environment for multi-bank holding companies is composed of the population of independent banks existing at a given point in time. A multi-bank holding company is defined as a holding company that owns two or more independent banks. Therefore, the carrying capacity of the banking environment for multi-bank holding companies is a function of the number of independent banks that are candidates for forming or being acquired by bank holding companies. As with any resource environment, the founding rate of multi-bank holding companies is expected to increase at a decreasing rate as the number of multi-bank holding companies (contingent on some average level of bank acquisitions) approaches the carrying capacity of the banking resource environment. The decreasing rate of multi-bank holding company foundings and acquisitions is attributable to high levels of competition for increasingly scarce banking resources in the form of attractive acquisition candidates. This is the point where additional increases in the multi-bank holding company form surpasses the carrying capacity of the resource environment and negative marginal returns are realized from addition bank acquisitions which causes the founding rate of multi-bank holding companies to decrease.

This is the classic non-monotonic function of density dependence on the founding rate of organizational forms within organizational fields (Hannan and Carroll 1992). The first-order effect of density on the founding rate of multi-bank holding companies is expected to be positive due to the increasing legitimation of the multi-bank holding company form. The second-order effect of density on the founding rate of the multi-bank holding company form is expected to be negative due to the effects of increasing competition for attractive acquisition targets. This indicates that the carrying capacity of resource environment is being approached, and competition effects begin to dominate the process of additional multi-bank holding companies foundings which causes the founding rate to decrease.

The founding rate is also expected to be effected by the number of foundings in prior years. The effect of prior foundings on the founding rate of an organizational form is known as rate dependence (Delacroix and Carroll 1983). The number of prior foundings provides a signal about potentially profitable opportunities existing in a resource environment. Therefore, according to the rate dependence notion, the founding rate of multi-bank holding companies is reliant on imitation and saturation processes. Successful forms are replicated by others through imitation. But as previously noted, resource spaces are limited, and a very large number of prior foundings is likely to reduce the number of adopters because of a saturation of the resource environment. Just as with density, the effects of prior foundings is expected to be non-monotonic. The first-order effect (imitation) of prior foundings increases the founding rate, and the second-order effect (saturation) of prior foundings decreases the founding rate.

In the late 1950s and early 1960s when the legitimacy of the multi-bank holding company was low to non-existent, the founding and acquisition rate of multi-bank holding companies was very low. In 1956, there were fewer than fifty multi-bank holding companies, and thirty-two states restricted branch banking. For over twenty years, legislation banning bank holding companies had been presented to Congress. In the early 1950s, Congress intervened in the Transamerica anti-trust case by disintegrating the multi-bank holding company empire. Banks promoting the multi-bank holding company form were relieved with passage of the Bank Holding Company Act of 1956 which regulated but did not ban multi-bank holding companies (Fisher 1961; Eccles 1982). The importance of the Bank Holding Company Act of 1956 was that it provided a clear legal definition of the multi-bank holding company form and specified regulatory powers. However, the legitimacy of the bank holding company form was questionable on two counts. One, the response of the Federal Reserve Board and the courts to bank acquisitions were unknown; and two, a comparison of the financial performance of multi-bank holding companies and their subsidiaries with the financial performance of independent banks was impossible because of a lack of history with the multi-bank holding company form.

The early adopters of the multi-bank holding company form (post-1956) were banking pioneers blazing the regulatory and litigation trail. Each bank acquisition established greater clarity regarding legal and performance criteria. Therefore, the legitimacy of the multi-bank holding company form in the 1960s can be rightly perceived as a function of increasing density. The founding rate of multi-bank holding companies is expected to increase at an increasing rate from 1956 through the 1970s as the multi-bank holding company gains legitimation. The increased legitimacy of the multi-bank holding company form in states that restrict branch banking is expected to result in the liberalization of state branch banking laws which occurs in the 1970s

The extremely high inflation rates of the late 1970s and early 1980s, the deregulation of banking, and the recession of the early 1980s are events whose cumulative impact caused substantial instability in financial markets in general and specifically in the financial performance of commercial banks in non-branch banking states. This environment of uncertainty and instability caused a continuing increase in the founding rate of multi-bank holding companies as banks attempted to adapt to the turbulent economic environment. However, at some point in the mid-1980s, the number of attractive candidates for bank acquisitions became scarce which would cause the founding rate of multi-bank holding companies to begin to decrease. Therefore, at the high density levels of the multi-bank holding company form in the mid-1980s, the founding rate of multi-bank holding companies is began to decrease. This is the predicted second-order effects of density and prior founding on founding rates.

An alternative perspective to understanding the legitimation of the multi-bank holding company form and corresponding changes in state branch banking laws is collective action theory. As previously noted, the institutions governing commercial banking are historically grounded in social and political environments, e.g. the political ideology of states' rights. The founding rate of multi-bank holding companies varies with degree of legitimacy, and the legitimacy of the multi-bank holding company form is contingent on complex social and political processes.

Institutional theory explains institutional origins and change in terms of the costs/benefits to individual parties and their relative bargaining power (Homans 1974; North 1990:83-88; Nee and Lian 1994; Nee and Ingram 1996). Banking institutions, whether at the level of the individual bank or at the level of state and federal laws, are designed to reduce uncertainty and to enhance the attainment of organizational objectives. Social structures are relatively enduring and are resistant to wholesale change. Change in social structures and their governing institutions generally occur in slow, incremental stages. Change in the governing institutions of commercial banking is initiated at the level of individual banks. If the bank holding company form proves successful, it diffuses to an ever greater proportion of the total population of commercial banks. Coupled with the diffusion of the multi-bank holding company form is the delegitimation of restrictive branch banking laws and the legitimation of liberalized branch banking laws. Change is branch banking regulations is evidence of the bargaining power of banks promoting the liberalization of branch banking opportunities relative to the power of those banks resisting change.

If the payoffs from organizing to change laws or regulations outweigh the costs of building and maintaining political organization, the probability of collective action designed to influence the political process increases (North 1990:89). The success of collective efforts is contingent on the ability of groups to mobilize and sustain participation. The key to successful political mobilization campaigns is the provision of selective incentives to mitigate free-riding (Olson 1965). The bank holding company associations recruit members by offering members valuable services such as coordination of state and federal legislative lobbying and the monitoring and dissemination of important information pertaining to regulations governing bank holding companies.

The collective action model assumes that political and economic environments are instituted by self-interested parties (Polanyi 1944; Fligstein 1996). The banking laws of the 1930s were designed to insure a safe and stable banking system. The restrictions on commercial banking were acceptable in lieu of the highly unstable banking and economic conditions of the 1930s. However, the return of prosperity in the post-WWII economy, the opportunity costs associated with the Depression era banking reforms increased for commercial bankers. The opportunity costs of commercial bankers increased with growing competition in financial markets coupled with limited expansion opportunities. The Bank Holding Company Act of 1956 effectively limited banks from engaging in business opportunities that were not closely related to banking, therefore, the only way to achieve increased payoffs in banking was to effect changes in state and federal banking laws.

The historical evolution of banking laws and regulations in the United States has been a contest between advocates of centralized, national banking and advocates of decentralized, local banking (Hammond 1957). The banking associations promoting the interests of multi-bank holding companies are advocates of centralized, nationwide banking, and the banking associations opposing multi-bank holding companies are committed to state control of banking. Therefore, the legitimation of the multi-bank holding company form and the repeal of state and federal restrictions on branch banking is not to be assumed a foregone conclusion. Throughout the nation's history, the formation of large nationwide banks have, for the most part, been successfully constrained by advocates of independent, localized banking.

Two banking associations at the forefront of advocating the repeal of branch banking restrictions are the Association of Reserve City Bankers and the Association of Bank Holding Companies. These two associations merged in 1993, and the current name is the Bankers Roundtable. The primary advocates of independent banks and continued state control of banking are the Independent Bankers Association and the Association of State Bank Regulators. The Association of State Bank Regulators was founded in 1907 to oppose federal encroachment of state bank regulatory powers by the Board of Governors of the Federal Reserve System which was established in 1913. The Independent Bankers Association was founded in 1933 with the explicit purpose of opposing the spread of bank holding companies.

The ability to successfully promote or resist change in restrictive branch banking laws is based on the political power differentials of competing banking interests. Institutional power is defined as the ability to control the material and human resources necessary to affect institutional outcomes (Lenski 1993:66). The great financial resources controlled by the large banks promoting multi-bank holding companies is offset by the great numerical superiority of small, independent banks. The American public has been receptive to the populist ideology of states' rights which is premised on ideas of decentralized power and the deconcentration of capital. Banks opposed to the spread of multi-bank holding companies have been able to tap this important political resource in mobilizing political opposition to bank holding companies (Fisher 1961). However, banking associations opposing multi-bank holding companies are confronted with a significant defection problem. The superior financial performance of multi-bank holding company subsidiaries and the generous premium accrued from acquisition are significant incentives to induce defection among independent banks. Therefore, the superior financial performance of multi-bank holding company subsidiaries causes an erosion in the power of independent banking associations as greater numbers of independent banks defect by seeking acquisition opportunities. This line of reasoning is consistent with the selection proposition.

I predict that liberalization of state branch banking laws is positively related to the number of multi-bank holding company foundings and acquisitions in a state. The number of multi-bank holding company foundings and acquisitions is an indicator of the power of multi-bank holding company advocates relative to their opponents. Also, the rate of change in branch banking laws is negatively should be associated with the number of small independent unit banks in a state. The numerical superiority of small banks in states should offset the political power of large banks since state legislators would be unwilling to alienate important power bases in widely dispersed regions of their states.

Economic crisis would be another cause of declining support for unit banking and an increase in the rate of change in branch banking laws. The analysis of bank failures concluded that bank failures were significantly related to independent banks and unit banking laws (see Table 4-11). This would strongly suggest that states experiencing economic crisis and large numbers of bank failures would be more likely to liberalize their branch banking laws in an effort to stem the tide of bank failures. The relationship between economic crisis and change in branch banking laws should definitely hold for oil states since they experienced not only a collapse in oil prices, but also, a collapse in real estate and agricultural markets which caused the number of bank failures to swell dramatically.

The banking laws of this country have been the result of a long and contentious struggle between rural farming interests and urban manufacturing interests (Hammond 1957). The Independent Banker's

Association was founded to protect the interests of rural main street banks from competitive encroachment by large urban banks. The political power of independent banks should be greater in states with the highest proportion of rural population, and the greatest resistance to change in restrictive branch banking laws should come from rural states. In contrast, the payoffs accruing collective political action by banks desiring geographic expansion should be greater in states with restrictive branch banking laws and with a high percentage of urban population. Over the observation period there has occurred a significant shift in population from urban centers to suburbs. In states experiencing a shift in population from cities to suburbs the costs of prohibitions on branch banking are high since banks cannot maintain their customer base if they are not allowed to open branch banks in the suburbs. Hence, political action to change unit banking laws is expected to occur in these states.

DATA AND METHODS

Data

The data for the density dependence analyses of the legitimation of the multi-bank holding company form and for the analysis of changes in state branch banking laws are the *Report of Income and Condition* and *Banking Holding Company File*, Federal Reserve System; *Annual Report*, Federal Deposit Insurance Corporation; and *Statistical Abstract of the United States*, U.S. Census Bureau.

Three separate analyses are performed. First, I specify two distinct models to test the density dependence effects of legitimation and competition on the multi-bank holding company founding rate. The dependent variable for the density dependence models is the transition rate of independent banks to lead banks of multi-bank holding companies. Second, I specify a model to test whether change in state branch laws precede or follow foundings and acquisitions of multi-bank holding companies. The dependent variable for the collective action model is the rate of change in branch banking laws.

When studying the establishment of a new population of organizations, the natural starting point is the founding date of the first organization and to measure the length of time between the founding of each additional organization. In this case, the usual method of analysis is to view founding of new organizations as an arrival process. The founding rates are estimated by the length of the time increments between successive foundings which is defined as the arrival of an additional organization. The unit of analysis is the population of new organizations, and past history or organizational characteristics are assumed unimportant since each new organizations history begins with its founding. Applying this approach to the study of multi-bank holding company foundings may not be appropriate since multi-bank holding companies are founded by banks that already exist.

Multi-bank holding companies are founded by an existing bank which becomes the lead bank of the new multi-bank holding company. In this case, the appropriate unit of analysis is the individual bank. Therefore, the founding rate of multi-bank holding companies is synonymous with the transition rate of independent banks and one-bank holding companies to the multi-bank holding company form. Rather than an arrival process, the transition of one form to another is viewed as an adaptation process. As discussed in Chapter 3, the multi-bank holding company form was not a viable option until after the Bank Holding Company Act of 1956 was enacted (Fisher 1961; Eccles 1982). Since the legitimation of the bank holding company form is the pivotal question being addressed, I use 1956 as beginning point in time for the population of multi-bank holding companies. In other words, from the time multi-bank holding companies were legally defined in 1956, what is the effect of density (proxy for legitimation and competition processes) on the founding rate of multi-bank holding companies? The increasing density or number of multi-bank holding companies is assumed to signify an increase in the legitimacy of the form which leads to the founding of additional multi-bank holding companies. The positive effect of density (legitimacy) on the founding rate of multi-bank holding companies is expected to have the greatest impact in the early stages of the history of the multi-bank holding company form.

The literature on the founding of new organizational populations lacks a study of the emergence of a new form from an already existing population of organizations. Whether findings regarding the effects of density will be similar for population level, arrival processes and individual level, adaptation processes is an interesting question to explore. The effects of density at both the population and individual level models should be identical over the long-term since the history of the organizational population has had the time to play itself out. But in the short-term, the case where the history of the organizational population is censored due to a lack of information regarding the future, the two methods of measuring foundings may produce different results. Population level analysis is premised on the availability of a complete history of the organizational population being studied. In this case, I have only a partial history on the population of multi-bank holding companies and the results have to be interpreted with this limitation in mind.

A listing of the independent variables for the density dependence models and their definitions are as follows:

Density Dependence—Legitimation and Competition

"log density"—the logarithm the cumulative number of transitions at the time of each transition. This is the first order density effect.

"density sq/1000"—the cumulative number of transitions at the time of each transition squared and divided by 1000. This is the second order density effect.

Rate Dependence—Imitation and Saturation

"prior foundings"—the observation period is divided into 36 annual periods and prior founding is measured as the cumulative number of multi-bank holding companies in the previous year.

"prior fnd. sq."—the number of prior founding squared.

Institutional Effects

"branch bk. st."—a dummy variable indicating banks in states with branch banking laws.

"lim. bran. st."—a dummy variable indicating banks in states with limited branch banking laws.

"fed. res. mem."—a dummy variable indicating Federal Reserve member banks.

Controls Variables

"interest rates"—an annual average of interest rates on three month Treasury bills.

"% st. pop. urb."—the percentage of a states' population that living in urban areas. Measured in ten year spans with mid-points 1960, 1970, 1980, 1990.

"st. per cap.inc."—a states' per capita income, constant 1987 dollars. Measured in ten year spans with mid-points 1960, 1970, 1980, 1990.

"region"—the region of the country that a bank is located; 1) north, 2) south, 3) midwest, 4) west.

I now discuss the specification of the collective action model which is presented an alternative explanation of the legitimation of the multi-bank holding company form as indicated by change in state branch banking laws. The collective action model is premised on the notion that the content of banking institutions governing specific structure of commercial are a function of power differentials among competing banking interests. Power is defined as the control of banking resources. The competing interests in commercial banking are those banks desiring unlimited growth opportunities and those banks desiring the status quo in 1956 of restricted banking markets. An interesting theoretical question raised by this analysis is whether changes in behavior precede change in rules governing behavior or if a change in rules precedes change in behaviors? In terms of commercial banking, do multi-bank holding company foundings and acquisitions precede changes in state branch banking laws or does change in state branch banking laws precede multi-bank holding company foundings and acquisitions?

The dependent variable for the analysis of branch banking laws is the date that change in state branch banking laws occurred between 1956 and 1991. Only those states restricting branch banking are included in this analysis since it assumed that the adoption of the multi-bank holding company form for the most part is a strategy designed to evade restrictions on branch banking. In 1956 there were thirty-two states with unit or limited branch banking laws. States that liberalize or repeal their restrictions on branch banking are viewed as contributing to the legitimation of the multi-bank holding company form since the adopters of multi-bank holding company are in essence promoting unlimited growth opportunities in the commercial banking sector. As noted in Chapter 3, the widespread adoption of multi-bank holding company form beginning the latter half of the 1960s was preceded by Congressional legislation defining the multi-bank holding company form, federal court ruling on bank mergers, and the establishment of bank merger guidelines by the Department of Justice and the Federal Reserve Board. These federal rulings and guidelines reduced the threshold of uncertainty and enabled innovative banks the opportunity to explore the feasibility of employing the multi-bank holding company form as a growth strategy. Federal quidelines gave the green light to market extension bank acquisitions as opposed to horizontal acquisitions which are designed to reduce competition in a market. The variables for the collective action model and their definitions are as follows:

Power

"mbhc founding ratio"—the ratio of lead banks of multi-bank holding companies to total banks in a state.

"acquisition ratio"—the ratio of banks acquired by MBHCs, excluding lead banks, to total banks in a state.

"small bank ratio"—the ratio of banks with less than $100 million in assets to the total number of banks in a state.

Crisis

"failed bank ratio"—the ratio of failed banks to total banks in a state.

"oil state"—a dummy variable indicating whether a bank is located in an oil state (Texas, Oklahoma, and Louisiana).

Controls

"interest rates"—an annual average of interest rates on three month Treasury bills.

"% st. pop. urb."—the percentage of a states' population living in urban areas. Measured in ten year spans with mid-points 1960, 1970, 1980, 1990.

"state inc/cap"—a states' per capita income, constant 1987 dollars. Measured in ten year spans with mid-points 1960, 1970, 1980, 1990.

"region"—the region of the country that a bank is located; 1) north, 2) south, 3) midwest, 4) west.

Descriptive statistics and zero order correlations for the models estimated are presented in Tables 6-1 and 6-2 respectively. The variables are categorized by the theoretical concepts operationalized by the independent variables.

Methods

The appropriate statistical method to use when studying stochastic processes with discrete state dependent variables and continuous time such as the transition of banks from state p to state z within the period t_0 - T is event history analysis (Tuma and Hannan 1984; Blossfeld, Hamerle and Mayer 1989). The transition rate for particular banks is expected to depend on observed and unobserved population heterogeneity, as well as, time. This pertains to the study of transition rates in state branch banking laws as well. The transition rates for all the analyses are expected to increase over time due to the increasing legitimation of the multi-bank holding company form. The effects of observed population heterogeneity on transition rates is captured by explanatory variables, and the effects of unobserved population heterogeneity and time on transition rates is reflected in the error terms. Since transition rates are non-negative a log-linear model of transition rates is estimated taking the form

$$\log r(t) = -\beta' \, x + u$$

where r(t) is the transition rate, and u is the disturbance term which implies that

$$r(t) = e^{-\beta' x} e^u.$$

The signs of the βs are negative because transition rates are calculated in terms of the time a case remains in state p before making a transition to state z. It follows that explanatory variables which increase the transition rate, decrease the amount of time a case is expected to remain in state p before making a transition to state z.

To explicitly test and control for the effects of time dependency and unobserved heterogeneity on bank transition rates, an exponential class of parametric event history models are specified. Within this class of models,

Table 6-1. Descriptive Statistics: Change in State Branch Banking
           Laws 1956-1991.

Variables:	Mean	Std.Dev.	Min.	Max.
Change Law	0.62	0.49	0.00	1.00
MBHC Founding Ratio	8.86	4.73	0.71	18.69
Acquisition Ratio	21.12	12.17	1.42	42.01
Small Bank Ratio	75.79	12.87	47.85	93.85
Failed Bank Ratio	4.21	5.47	0.00	24.92
Oil State	0.03	0.18	0.00	1.00
Interest Rate	6.46	2.24	1.73	14.02
% St.Pop.Urban	64.28	19.75	23.90	99.10
State Inc/Capita	15153.80	2370.00	11157.00	21636.00
Region	2.16	0.88	1.00	4.00

N = 32

****

Table 6-2. Zero Order Correlations.

Variables:	(1)	(2)	(3)	(4)	(5)	(6)	(7)	(8)	(9)
1) Change Law	---								
2) MBHC Fnds	-.52	---							
3) Acquis	-.09	.42	---						
4) Small Bnks	-.11	-.04	-.24	---					
5) Failed Bnks	-.36	.17	-.28	.25	---				
6) Oil State	.13	.10	.03	.05	.01	---			
7) % Pop.Urb.	.40	-.14	.29	-.59	-.19	.16	---		
8) Inc/Capita	.40	-.08	.29	-.50	-.35	-.05	.69	---	
9) Region	-.23	.15	-.11	.75	.39	-.03	-.45	-.35	---

N = 32

the baseline model is the constant rate exponential model. The exponential model assumes a time invariant (constant) transition rate for all cases at risk of having an event, and no effects are attributed to unobserved population heterogeneity. Unobserved population heterogeneity is analogous to the effects of omitted explanatory variables in linear regression models. The exponential model takes the estimation form

$$\log r(t) = -\beta'x + W$$

where r(t) is the transition rate and the disturbance W has an extreme value distribution.[1] Since it is highly probable that the transition rates of banks are not constant over the observation period, an inter-related class of models (the Weibull, gamma, and generalized gamma models) are estimated which have as special cases the exponential model. The general form of the exponential family of models takes the estimation form

$$\log r(t) = -\beta^*x + \sigma W$$

where r(t) is the transition rate, $\beta^* = -\beta\sigma$, and the disturbance term W has an extreme value distribution. The Weibull model includes a scale parameter which tests and controls for the effects of time dependency, the gamma model contains a shape parameter which tests and controls for the effects of unobserved heterogeneity, and the generalized gamma model tests and controls for both time dependency and unobserved heterogeneity by including scale, q, and shape, k, parameters. For the Weibull and generalized gamma models which contain a scale for time dependency, if $0 < q < 1$ the transition rate is monotonic decreasing, and if $q > 1$ the transition rate is monotonic increasing. If $q = 1$ the Weibull model reduces to the exponential model. For the gamma and generalized gamma models which contain a shape parameter for unobserved heterogeneity, if $k \neq 1$ the presence of unobserved heterogeneity is indicated. The generalized gamma model has as special cases the exponential ($q = 1$, $k = 1$), the Weibull ($q \neq 1$, $k = 1$), and the gamma ($q = 1$, $k \neq 1$).

In addition to the exponential family of event history models, a log-logistic model is estimated to test for non-monotonic time dependency. The log-logistic model is not included in the exponential family of event history estimators since it does not reduce to the exponential model. However, if time dependency is indicated by the Weibull or generalized gamma models, the log-logistic model can be used to test whether the form of time dependency is monotonic or non-monotonic. For the log-logistic model, if the scale parameter q is less than or equal to 1 the transition rate is a monotonic, decreasing function of time, and if the scale parameter q is greater than 1 the form of the transition rate is first increasing and then decreasing. Hence, the transition rate is a non-monotonic function of time.

The event history results presented in the tables are the transformed coefficients of the explanatory variables. The signs of the explanatory variables have been reversed so that the longer the period of time that a case remains in state p the lower the transition rate. Also, the reported coefficients have been transformed to account for the effects of time dependency. The coefficients are transformed by taking $\beta = -(1/\sigma)\beta^*$ and by taking $q = 1/\sigma$ where σ is the estimated value of the scale parameter, and q is the transformed scale parameter reported in the tables. The individual bank, density dependence models presented in Table 6-4 are estimated with the exponential model only because of the problem of estimating the effects of banks founded post-1956. This is not a problem with the population level, density models since the timing of transitions is modeled as an inter-arrival process such that time is measured in terms of the time intervals between successive transitions.

Since the estimation equation for transition rates is a log-linear model, the anti-logs of the coefficients of the explanatory variables are interpreted as a multiplier effect. When the transformed coefficients of continuous explanatory variables are exponentiated, they are interpreted as the percentage increase or decrease in the transition rate for a one unit increase in the explanatory variable. The exponentiation of transformed coefficients of dummy variables is interpreted as the percentage increase or decrease in transition rates for the presence of an attribute versus the absence of the attribute. The event history results presented in Tables 6-3, 6-4, and 6-6 are the un-exponentiated transformed coefficients. In the findings and discussion sections, the results discussed are the exponentiated or the multiplier effect (percentage increase/decrease) of explanatory variables on bank transition rates.

The likelihood ratio test is an appropriate goodness-of-fit measure for the event history models (Kalbfleisch and Prentice 1980:48). The likelihood ratio test,

$$R(\theta) = -2(\log L_1 - \log L_2),$$

can be used to evaluate the comparative fit of nested event history models since the asymptotic distribution of $-2\log R(\theta)$ is chi-square with q degrees of freedom where q is the difference in the number of constraints between the models being evaluated.

FINDINGS

The results for the population level, density dependence models are presented in Table 6-3. While the coefficient estimates vary somewhat in magnitude, the signs and significance levels are the identical across the event history models. The presence of unobserved heterogeneity and non-monotonic time dependence is indicated by the scale and shape parameters of the log-logistic and generalized gamma models respectively.

As predicted, the first-order effect of density is positive, and the second-order effect of density is negative. Both coefficients are statistically significant from zero. This supports the hypothesis that the multi-bank holding company founding rate increases in the early stages of its history due to increasing legitimacy, but decreases in the latter stages as the carrying capacity of the resource environment is approached.

The effect of prior foundings is also as predicted. The first-order effect of prior foundings is positive and statistically significant, and the second-order is negative and statistically significant. These two findings imply that in the early history of an organizational population imitation/learning processes increase the founding rate, but as the population of new organizations matures an increase in prior foundings indicates a saturation of the resource niche and causes the founding rate to decrease.

The period effects suggest a cyclic process of foundings. A non-monotonic founding rate is also implied by the scale parameter of the log-logistic model. Multi-bank holding company foundings increase in the late sixties, decrease in the mid-1970s, increase in the late-1970s and early-1980s, and then decrease in the late-1980s. The increase in the 1960s is attributable to the establishment of merger guidelines. The decrease in the 1970s is a result of the uncertainty created by the oil embargoes. The increase in the late-1970s and early-980s is a response to bank de-regulation

Table 6-3. Population Level Density Dependence Models of Multi-Bank Holding Company Foundings 1956-1991. Waiting Time Measured as Interval Between Successive Foundings. Generalized Gamma Event History and Log-Logistic Models.

Variables:	Generalized Gamma			Log-Logistic Model
	Model 1	Model 2	Model 3	
Constant	-5.470**	-6.060**	-5.724**	-9.992**
Density				
Log Density	0.370**	0.517**	0.290**	0.570**
Density Sq/1000	---	-1.4E-4**	-1.6E-4**	-3.8E-4*
Imitation				
Prior Foundings	---	---	0.014**	0.033**
Prior Fnd. Sq.	---	---	-3.5E-5**	-9.4E-5**
Controls				
Interest Rate	-0.019	-0.043*	0.018	0.080
Period Effects				
Period 2 (1967-1991)	-2.3E-4	-0.023	-0.008	0.187
Period 3 (1973-1991)	-0.004	0.051	-0.064	-0.886**
Period 4 (1980-1991)	0.772**	0.708**	0.087	0.070
Period 5 (1986-1991)	-0.393**	-0.365**	-0.074	-0.152
Scale	0.700**	0.703**	0.715**	1.191**
Shape	0.361**	0.363**	0.418**	---
-2 Log L Ratio	130.2**	13.0**	43.8**	---
df	1	1	2	---

** -- $p < .01$; * -- $p < .05$ # Foundings = 1758

and strong returns on equity in banking. The decrease in the late-1980s is a reaction to the deteriorating financial performance of banks and to the volatile economic climate.

The results for the individual bank level, density dependence models are presented in Table 6-4. The results are very similar to the population level results except for second-order effects of density. Note that both the first-order and second-order effects of density are positive and statistically significant. The second-order effect of density is positive which means that competition effects are not yet dominant. The interpretation is that the multi-bank holding company founding rate increases in the early stages due to legitimacy and continues to increase over the observation period. I believe that this is a more accurate representation of what is occurring than the results of the population level, density dependence model. Bank holding company foundings peaked in the mid-1980s and are still occurring at relatively high levels in the late-1980s and early 1990s. Based on the number of independent banks and one-bank holding companies still in existence, it is plausible to conclude that the carrying capacity of the bank holding company niche has not yet been reached, and therefore, processes of legitimation are still operative. This contradictory finding does not imply that the theory of density dependence is wrong since the data is censored in that a complete organizational history is not captured by the observation period. The differences in estimates is an artifact of the difference in time scales used to estimate the founding rates. The inter-arrival, time intervals of the population model reflect the short time intervals between foundings in the late-1970s through the early-1980s, and the longer time intervals between foundings in the late-1980s is what produces the negative second-order effect of density. On the other hand, the bank level model measures all time intervals in terms of duration from 1956. This measurement scheme places the peak period of foundings in the latter part of the observation period which produces the positive second-order effect of density.

The positive first-order and negative second order effects of prior foundings on the founding rates of multi-bank holding companies are indicators of imitation and saturation processes respectively. Both estimates are statistically significant. These results are very similar to the results of the population level model. The positive first-order effect of recent prior foundings suggests that the imitation processes increase the founding rate of multi-bank holding companies. The negative second-order effect implies that

Table 6-4. Individual Bank Density Dependence Models of Multi-Bank
Holding Company Foundings, 1956-1991. Exponential Event
History Models.

Variables:	Model 1	Model 2	Model 3	Model 4
Constant	-21.566*	-17.531**	-17.343**	-17.482**
Density				
Log Density	1.486**	0.460**	0.531**	0.372**
Density Sq/1000	1.4E-4*	2.8E-4**	3.4E-4**	2.7E-4**
Imitation				
Prior Foundings	--	0.039**	0.038**	0.042**
Prior Fnd. Sq.	--	-9.8E-5**	-9.3E-5**	-1.1E-4**
Institutions				
Branch Bk. St.	--	--	-0.723**	-0.844**
Lim. Bran. St.	--	--	-0.868**	-0.861**
Fed. Res. Mem.	--	--	0.258**	0.215**
Controls				
Interest Rates	0.069**	0.049**	0.045**	0.037**
% St.Pop.Urb.	--	--	--	-0.002
State Inc/Cap.	--	--	--	1.2E-4**
Region	--	--	--	-0.121**
Period Effects				
Period 2 (1967-1991)	0.735**	0.706**	0.591**	0.526**
Period 3 (1973-1991)	-0.947**	-0.539**	-0.669**	-0.665**
Period 4 (1980-1991)	-0.780**	-0.785**	-0.837**	-0.835**
Period 5 (1986-1991)	-3.251**	-3.595**	-3.374**	-3.377**
-2 Log L Ratio	2424.1**	784.8**	270.8**	59.9**
df	2	2	3	3

** -- $p < .01$ # of Transitions = 1758
* -- $p < .05$ Censored Sub-Spells = 448693

in the periods following a large number of multi-bank holding company foundings the founding rate decreases. These results are consistent with the data presented in Table 4-6 which shows a decrease in the number of multi-bank holding company foundings in the late-1980s after much activity in the early and mid-1980s.

The institutional effects of state branch banking laws and Federal Reserve membership are very similar to the event history results reported in Chapter 4. These results provide further support for the hypothesis that state branch banking laws are important predictors of bank holding company activity. Also, the coefficients for the control variables are similar to those reported in Chapter 4.

The analysis of change in state branch banking laws produces some surprising results. In 1956, there were 32 states with unit and limited branch banking laws. It is these states that are being analyzed to assess the de-legitimation of restrictive branch banking laws over the 1956-1989 observation period. A summary of change in state branch banking laws is presented in Table 6-5. Over the observation period the number of branch banking states increased by 10, and the number of unit banking states decreased by 13. At the beginning of the observation period 32 states had some form of branch banking restrictions, and by the end of observation period 22 states had some form of branch banking restrictions. But what is the cause of change in branch banking laws? The prediction is that as the number of multi-bank holding companies and bank acquisitions in a state increases, the support for the repeal of branch banking restrictions increases which leads to change in state branch banking laws.

The event history results for change in state branch banking law model are presented in Table 6-6. The multi-bank holding company ratio variable has a statistically significant effect on change in branch banking laws, but the effect is negative which is opposite the predicted effect. A one percent increase in the ratio of multi-bank holding companies in a state is associated with a 50 decrease in the probability of change in its branch banking law. This finding implies that change in branch banking laws precedes the founding of multi-bank holding companies. This is consistent with the data presented in Table 4-7 which shows that most bank holding company activity occurs in limited branch banking states. But keep in mind that many of the limited branch banking states were originally unit banking states. The inference being that in unit banking states, branch banking restrictions were

Table 6-5. State Branch Banking Laws: Totals by Type and Year

	1961	1976	1983	1989
Branch Banking	19	20	23	29
Limited Branch Banking	15	16	17	18
Unit Banking	17	15	11	4

****

Table 6-6. Change in State Branch Banking Laws 1956-1991. Weibull Event History Models.

Variables:	Model 1	Model 2	Model 3
Intercept	-39.25**	-42.20**	-74.63**
Power			
MBHC Founding Ratio	-0.35**	-0.38**	-0.40**
Acquisition Ratio	0.05**	0.04*	-0.01
Small Bank Ratio	-0.02	-0.02	0.06
Crisis			
Failed Bank Ratio	---	-0.10*	-0.10*
Oil State	---	2.37**	2.02*
Controls			
Interest Rate	---	---	0.01
% State Pop. Urban	---	---	0.04
State Income/Capita	---	---	3.6E-4**
Region	---	---	-0.50
Scale	0.23**	0.21**	0.14**
(-2) Log L Ratio	---	7.70*	15.44**
df	3	2	4
** -- p < .05; * -- p < .10			N = 32

liberalized and banks created branch banks through the formation of multi-bank holding companies and bank acquisition rather than establishing branch banks de novo.

In some unit banking states, not only were branch banks prohibited, but also, de facto branch banking through multi-bank holding company acquisitions were prohibited (Brown 1983). Before multi-bank holding companies could be founded, unit banking laws had to be changed to limited branch banking laws. This interpretation is consistent with the collective action hypothesis that in those states where branch banking opportunities are totally denied, incentives exist for banks desiring growth to invest in political action to change prohibitive branch banking laws. Once branch banking restrictions are liberalized, banks are able to achieve geographic expansion by forming multi-bank holding companies and acquiring banks.

This line of reasoning is consistent with the findings related to the effects of the variables failed bank ratio, oil state, and state per capita income. The incentive to achieve growth through the liberalization of state branch banking would be greatest in wealthier states where the returns to geographic expansion would be greatest. A $1,000 increase in a state's per capita income translates into a 43 percent higher probability that the state changes its branch banking law. On the other hand, in states experiencing economic uncertainty, as indicated by the ratio of failed banks, decreases the probability of change in branch banking law by 10 percent. The incentive to invest in political action to liberalize branch banking laws is not as great in states with high ratio of failed banks because of greater uncertainty regarding potential returns. This was not true in oil states where the number of bank failures created a crisis of substantial proportions. In these states, a liberalization of branch banking laws was necessary to stabilize the banking environment. The effects of the other two power variables, acquisition and small bank ratios, are not statistically significantly. These findings suggest that it is not the relative power of competing interests but the structure of incentives that is the critical factor in determining the rate of change in branch banking laws.

The Association of Bank Holding Companies is an important advocate for multi-bank holding companies over the observation period.[2] According to the Association's promotional literature "The purpose of the Association is to provide a forum for the top officers of member companies to discuss industry developments, to formulate legislative and regulatory policy positions. . . . " The 160 member banks of the Association which are located in all 50 states control approximately $1.5 trillion in assets and 75 percent of the banking business in the United States. The Association has a substantial budget, a legal staff, lobbyists, and researchers. The long-run objective of the organization was to win Congressional authorization of interstate banking which was achieved in the fall of 1994. Another significant banking association promoting the interests of multi-bank holding companies is the Association of Reserve City Bankers. The Reserve City Bankers Association is an established, elite banking association whose membership is limited to banks with assets of at least a billion dollars. These two organizations are formidable advocates of state and federal banking regulations favorable to the interests of multi-bank holding companies.

Opposition to bank holding companies is organized primarily by the Independent Banker's Association founded in the midwest in the 1930s. The purpose of this association is to protect the autonomy of small rural banks from the competition with large urban banks. Therefore, it is not surprising that the four states that still had unit banking laws in 1989 were midwestern states with large farm constituencies (see Table 4-1). A former bank president in a state that changed its branch banking law in the mid-1980s stated in a personal interview that independent bankers were very successful in their legislative efforts in opposition to the ascendancy of multi-bank holding companies in the 1950s and 1960s but by the mid-1970s the tide began to turn in favor of multi-bank holding companies.

On a final note, a Weibull event history model is estimated because a Weibull model is the best fit to the data according to the likelihood ratio tests with other estimators. The scale parameter is less than 1 which indicates that the rate of change in branch banking laws is declining over the observation period. This finding is consistent with the data since most of the changes in branch banking laws occurred in the mid- to late-1970s.

DISCUSSION AND SUMMARY

An interesting picture emerges concerning the legitimation of the multi-bank holding company form from the selection and collective action analyses. Both models provide evidence that the legitimation of the multi-bank holding company form and change in state branch banking laws is occurring in a punctuated or incremental fashion. The interpretation of the selection models premised on the notion of density dependence implies that the legitimation of the multi-bank holding company form is associated with the increasing density of the form. As the form gains legitimacy, the form's founding rate increases. The increasing density of the multi-bank holding form provided a signal to bank managers and shareholders that growth opportunities existed through adoption of the form. Increased density also provided a larger pool of information with which to compare and evaluate the effects of bank structure on financial performance. The legitimacy of the multi-bank holding company form was promoted by the enhanced profitability as measured by the higher returns on assets and equity of their subsidiaries in non-branch banking states. In addition, the legitimation of the form accruing from improved financial performance of subsidiaries was augmented by the generous premiums in excess of book value paid shareholders of acquired banks for accumulated goodwill.

The findings reinforce the conceptualization of legitimation as a process that occurs over time rather than at any particular point in time. The positive second-order effect of density in the bank level, density dependence model signifies that legitimation effects is influencing the multi-bank holding company founding rate throughout the observation period. The multi-bank holding company founding rate is expected to begin to decrease when the carrying capacity of the bank holding company resource environment is attained. This would be indicated by a negative second-order effect of density, and the positive second-order effect of density in Table 6-4 insinuates that the carrying capacity of the resource environment to sustain addition multi-bank holding companies has not yet been reached.

The population level, density dependence models which are measured in terms of the inter-arrival times between successive event occurrences indicate that the effects of density on the multi-bank holding company founding rate in non-monotonic as evidenced by the positive first-order and negative second-order effects of density (see Table 6-3). Not all banks are equally viable candidates for founding a multi-bank holding company due to resource constraints or preferences. Likewise, not all banks are equally attractive candidates for acquisition due to variation in markets, performance, and capital structure. Multi-bank holding company foundings and acquisitions are expected to occur in cycles in response to changes in bank resource environment. The cycles are bounded by the declining marginal returns of additional multi-bank holding company foundings and acquisitions. The founding and acquisition rates of multi-bank holding companies declines as the number of viable candidates for multi-bank holding company foundings and acquisitions become scarce. These conclusions are supported by the positive first-order and negative second-order effects of recent prior founding.

In understanding the process of change occurring in commercial banking, it is important to note that over five thousand one-bank holding companies and over three thousand independent banks still exist in 1991 which indicates that the carrying capacity of the bank resource environment has not yet been reached. A plausible interpretation of the decreasing founding rate in the late 1980s is that the analysis is capturing a temporary lull in the diffusion of the multi-bank holding company form due to the unstable banking environment of that period. The founding rate of multi-bank holding companies may increase again with the return of prosperity in the early 1990s. Therefore, it is difficult to make inferences about selection processes with a right censored organizational history. The large number of independent banks and one-bank holding companies in 1991 suggests that a punctuated selection process is occurring and that a longer observation period is required to capture the true nature of the selection process.

The cyclic interpretation is provided additional support by the period effects. The period 1956-1966 is a period where multi-bank holding company founding and acquisition activity is low due to anti-trust challenges of bank acquisitions. With increasingly legal clarity and the enactment of the Bank Merger Act of 1966, the multi-bank holding company founding rate begins to increase in the mid-1960s through the early 1970s. The economic disruptions and uncertainties imposed by international petroleum politics in the 1970s caused a slowdown in multi-bank holding company activity. Economic adjustments to the changing price structures of input factors attributable to an explosion in petroleum prices caused high inflation and an tremendous increase in loanable funds held by banks. Coupled with bank deregulation and relaxation of anti-trust enforcement, the excess cash reserves resulted in a rapid increase in multi-bank holding company activity in the late 1970s and early 1980s. Multi-bank holding company activity declines markedly in the mid- to late-1980s with the onset of regional economic and banking crises caused by collapses in real estate, agricultural, and energy markets.

I believe these results support the conclusion that the effects of legitimation on the founding rate of multi-bank holding companies is dominant over the limited observation period of this analysis. It took ten years for court tested bank merger and acquisition guidelines to be defined with the enactment of the Bank Merger Act of 1966. Over the next fourteen years, multi-bank holding company foundings and acquisitions were modest and relatively constant. This period can be characterized as a time when first-movers began to innovate with the multi-bank holding company form as a means for evading branch banking restrictions and realizing first-mover advantages and returns if successful. By the 1980s and onset of bank deregulation, the financial performance of the multi-bank holding companies founded in the 1960s and 1970s could readily be assessed and based on the strength of their financial performance. This initiate the emerging legitimacy of the multi-bank holding company form, and it began to diffuse rapidly in the late 1970s forward.

While I do not have bank data beyond 1991, interviews with staff of the Independent Bankers Association indicates that the founding rate of multi-bank holding companies may be increasing in the 1990s as smaller banks merge to realize scale economies and to position themselves financially to resist takeovers by regional and national multi-bank holding companies. The endorsement of the multi-bank holding company form by the Independent Bankers Association in the 1990s as a method to improve the financial performance of small banks is further indication that legitimation processes are still driving processes of change within the commercial banking community.

An intriguing issue in the study of structural and institutional change in organizational environments is the procedural question concerning whether change is initiated by a change in practices or whether a change in practices is preceded by changes in formal rules and regulations. In the preceding discussion, the legitimacy of the multi-bank holding company is evaluated in terms of increasing density. This implies that the process of institutionalization is predicated on the prevalence of prior changes in practices. In other words, an innovative practice becomes institutionalized or legitimated as it becomes the taken-for-granted. It follows that change in formal rules and regulations occupies a higher level of change and follows changes in practices. Following this logic, it was predicted that change in restrictive branch banking laws are preceded by the prevalence of multi-bank holding company foundings and acquisitions in a state.

The results of the event history analysis of change in state branch banking laws contradicts the prediction that multi-bank holding company foundings and acquisitions precede change in branch banking laws. The ratio of multi-bank holding companies in a state has a negative effect on change in branch banking laws, and the ratio of bank acquisitions has no effect. Research findings similar to these were obtained by Strang and Bradburn (1993) in their analysis of state enabling legislation for health maintenance organizations (HMOs). The findings of Strang and Bradburn indicated that state HMO enabling legislation preceded the founding of HMOs. Also, states with large HMO enrollments were slower to pass enabling legislation. If institutional change is not caused by the cumulative effect of prior behavioral change, what does account for institutional change? Delacroix, Swaminathan, and Solt (1989) maintain that organizational populations emerge in environments that can be either institutionally supportive or hostile. Other empirical studies demonstrate the role of organizational associations in controlling hostile or potentially hostile institutional environments (Starr 1982; Torres 1988; DiMaggio 1991; Brint and Karabel 1991). These studies support the contention that a collective action model can be used to clarify the relationship between the adoption of the multi-bank holding company form and changes in state branch banking laws.

Collective action theory includes in the calculation of opportunity costs the costs of creating rule change.[3] When the opportunity costs of foregoing profitable opportunities prohibited by law, including the costs of creating rule change, is greater than the rewards associated with action in compliance to the rules then it is to be expected that interested parties will join together and attempt to change the rules (North 1990:87). The same logic pertains to assessing the likelihood that affected interests will act collectively to resist a proposed rule changes. These collective action propositions are consistent with the observed changes in restrictive branch banking laws.

In those states where the multi-bank holding company strategy to achieve entry into new markets through bank acquisitions went unopposed by state bank regulators, there were no gains in returns from investing in political action to change branch banking laws. Therefore, it follows that the rate of change in restrictive branch banking laws will be lower in states with high multi-bank holding company ratios. On the other hand, in states where restrictions on branch banking are strictly enforced, regardless of whether expansion be through the establishment of de novo branch banks or acquisitions, the payoff for investing in collective political action to change branch banking laws is high. Therefore, the rate of change in restrictive branch banking laws is expected to be greater in states with low multi-bank holding company ratios. This explanation is consistent with the finding presented in Table 5-6.

However, this explanation fails to explain how banks wanting change in restrictive branch banking laws are able to overcome opposition to change. The data through 1991 clearly indicates that the number of banks remaining independent, including one-bank holding companies, greatly exceed the number of banks associated with multi-bank holding companies. It is fair to assume that the large numerical superiority of independent banks can potentially be translated into significant political power capable of offsetting the superior resources of the large banks desiring change in branch banking laws. Therefore, how does change in restrictive branch banking laws occur in the face of such formidable opposition.

The answer to this dilemma is framed within the context of the free-rider problem (Olson 1965).[4] Generally the largest and most influential banks possess the resources and have the most to gain by liberalizing branch banking laws. Due to the small number of large banks needed to form and sustain multi-bank holding company associations, the associations are not susceptible to significant free-riding problems. The relatively homogeneous membership base of multi-bank holding company associations minimizes the potential for intra-organizational conflict which maximizes the commitment of members to political strategies. The high degree of consensus within small, homogeneous groups increases the perception among individual members of the efficacy of fully participating in the attainment of collective objectives. Also, they are able to effectively monitor and enforce member compliance at a relatively low cost, and thereby, to effectively mount and sustain political action. In addition, the small number of members enhances the association's ability to provide meaningful selective benefits to their members in the form of research, legal assistance, and political lobbying.

Collective action is more difficult to sustain and free-riding more problematic in large groups with a diverse membership base. These are the conditions confronting associations representing the interests of independent banks. Since both bank managers and shareholders of independent banks are confronted with potentially significant payoffs by forming or affiliating with a multi-bank holding company, the incentive structure for sustaining collective is more complex in the case of independent banks compared to multi-bank holding companies. Multi-bank holding companies are able to encourage the defection of independent banks by offering continued control and autonomy to acquired banks. In addition, they are able to offer substantial premiums over book value of bank shares for accumulated goodwill. Therefore, it is not surprising that opposition to multi-bank holding companies has eroded and liberalization of restrictive branch banking laws has occurred over the observation period.

The extent to which the multi-bank holding company form diffuses within and across state boundaries is likely to be a function of the ability of multi-bank holding companies to continue to satisfy the preferences of bank managers and shareholders. As long as the returns to acquired banks are greater than the returns that can be expected by remaining independent, the defection of independent banks can be expected to continue. The analyses of financial performance in Chapter 5 found that very large banks experience diminishing returns associated with scale and scope economies which is consistent with a large body of research on bank financial performance. Therefore, the final extent to which the multi-bank holding company form will restructure commercial banking is uncertain.

Centralized, nationwide banking has been the objective of some bankers since the nation's founding but were constrained from doing so until very recently (Hammond 1957). The bank holding company has been the means adopted by bankers to achieve statewide, regional, and national growth in lieu of state and federal laws restricting intra- and inter-state branch banking. The bank holding company form allows banks to rapidly establish new markets through the acquisition of established independent banks. Also, the multi-bank holding company form enables banks to maintain intra- and inter-state customer relations with regional and national manufacturing and retail firms through the establishment of limited service non-bank subsidiaries. It is very plausible that the bank multi-bank holding company form was strictly designed as a strategy to evade restrictive bank regulations and that the ultimate goal is the formation of integrated, nationwide, full-financial service banks. This is beginning to increasingly occur with the implementation of inter-state banking regulations.

In 1956, thirty-two states restricted intra-state branch banking and all fifty states prohibited inter-state banking but by 1989 twenty-two states restricted intra-state branch banking and forty-six states provided for some form of inter-state branch banking. The most noteworthy aspect of change in state and federal branch banking laws over the thirty-six year observation period is the incremental nature of the change. On the one hand, there is a perception of tremendous change, while on the other hand there is a perception of great stability and little overall change. There are elements of truth to both perceptions. Stability and incremental change is to be expected since social structures and their governing institutions are defined as being relatively stable and resistant to change. But what are the dynamics governing change in state branch banking laws?

It is clear that state intra- and inter-state branch laws have been liberalized and that the multi-bank holding company form has momentum for further restructuring the banking landscape. It is also evident that a large number of moderate sized one-bank holding companies are maintaining a strong financial performance levels and have the potential to preserve the dual state/federal banking system in the United States. It is left for future research to document the processes of change that are occurring in the structure and institutions of commercial banking in the United States.

NOTES

1. When logarithmic data is used the error term is often approximated by an extreme value distribution (Blossfeld, Hamerle, and Mayer 1989:36-39).

2. In 1993 the Association of Bank Holding Companies (160 member banks) was acquired by the Reserve City Bankers Association (88 member banks) and the new organization is named the Bankers Roundtable. Most members of the Reserve City Bankers Association were also members of the Association of Bank Holding Companies.

3. Opportunity costs are the sum total of payoffs associated with alternative courses of action once a particular course of action has been chosen. The payoff related to a course of action which is contingent on creating a rule change must be adjusted to account for the costs of creating a rule change. Hence, the costs of creating a rule change is a component of opportunity costs.

4. The free-rider problem is associated with the provision of public goods. A public good such as branch banking laws is a good whose benefits are non-excludable. Once a branch banking law is enacted all banks share in the benefits

accruing from the law. Why should a rational banker whose participation in collective action to maintain branch banking restrictions has an insignificant effect on the outcome pay the costs of participating in collective action, and thereby, free-rides on the participation of others and enjoys the benefits without sharing in the costs.

CHAPTER 7

Conclusions

This institutional analysis of commercial banking has successfully explained some of the significant changes that occurred in commercial banking over the observation period. Unique to most contemporary sociological studies of organizations, this analysis demonstrates the merits of explicitly modeling human agency. Traditional sociological theories of organizations generally emphasize the normative, mimetic, or coercive effects of the institutional environment on organizational behavior (DiMaggio and Powell 1991). According to the traditional perspective, the genesis of organizational change is attributed to exogenous environmental factors such as economic crisis, state action, or the dynamics of competing institutional logics (Powell 1988; Fligstein 1990). This study demonstrates the merits of acknowledging the effects of strategic action on social dynamics. Strategic action is definitely an important source of change in organizational environments. Organizations, like individuals, strategically plan their futures, and part of the strategic planning process involves considering the constraints imposed by the formal and informal institutional framework. Most of the time, organizational behavior is in conformity with the prevailing institutions, but at other times, innovative action is undertaken with the explicit purpose of changing the prevailing institutional environment. Therefore, it is important to consider the potential effects emanating from the interaction of strategic action within the confines of formal and informal institutional frameworks. The results of this study have provided a textbook example of how strategies designed by banks wanting to pursue growth opportunities not available to them because of the prevailing banking regulations evolved to create substantial change in the structure and institutions of commercial banking.

The analyses present clear evidence of the efficacy of the multi-bank holding company form as a means of evading branch banking restrictions. The initiation of this growth strategy took place well in advance of any environmental crisis or state action. In fact the regulatory and legal groundwork for the multi-bank holding company form was initiated in a period of growth, profitability, and stability in commercial banking. Brewing on the horizon were indications of an impending storm arising from increasing competition in financial markets, and in response to the warning signs, advocates of the multi-bank holding company form set in motion a plan of action. This is strategic behavior embedded within an institutional and competitive environment.

The strategies enacted by commercial bankers and the ensuing changes in the structure and institutions of commercial banking can readily be understood in terms of the changing incentive structure imposed by the Depression era banking laws coupled with state restrictions on branch banking. The multi-bank holding company strategy is not a radical change in organizational structure and does not exact radical change in banking practices. In fact, the use of the multi-bank holding company form enabled its advocates the opportunity to blunt opposition by offering acquired banks semi-control and autonomy over local banking operations. The process of change brought about by multi-bank holding companies has been incremental, and opponents have been successful in devising defensive strategies to protect the integrity of independent banking through the use of the one-bank holding company form.

The most significant change over the past forty years in the structure of commercial banking is the demise of unit banking regulations. Whereas, a third of the states had unit banking laws at the beginning of the observation period, no state has a unit banking law today. While movement toward statewide and interstate branch banking has definitely occurred, the movement has not been wholesale for approximately forty percent of states still have some form of limits on intra-state branch banking and inter-state banking is being regulated by the states through the formation of regional regulatory banking compacts.

While the large money center and urban banks have tremendous financial and political resources at their disposal, independent banks have been able to effectively mobilize their superior numerical strength in state and federal regulatory arenas to maintain the dual state/federal banking system of the United States. What the future holds as nationwide branch banking becomes a reality is an empirical question to be answered by further research. There is evidence that smaller banks are forming multi-bank holding companies in the 1990s to strengthen their ability to compete with larger banks which would signify a possible resurgence of multi-bank holding company foundings in the 1990s (Personal Interviews). Also, many mergers of multi-bank holding companies have been prominently covered in the press in the mid-1990s which would signify that competitive processes are thinning the ranks of the largest multi-bank holding companies. Of particular interest is the finding of diseconomies of scale for the very largest banks. This finding is consistent with a growing body of bank research. In contrast, moderately large banks have the best performance in terms of return on assets and equity. The obvious question for the large nationwide banking networks being built with a holding company structure is how are the negative effects of scale on bank performance being mitigated?

The banking crisis of the late-1980s and the large number of bank failures provided the motivation for me to do this study. At the time, there was considerable concern that commercial banking would experience a collapse similar to the collapse of the savings and loan industry. Anything but occurred in commercial banking, and commercial banking in the 1990s is one of the most profitable of all American industries. This study has clarified for me the reasons why commercial banking as an industry survived the turbulent 1980s relatively unscathed. The legitimation of the multi-bank holding company form in the 1960s and 1970s fortuitously placed the industry in a position to absorb the many under performing banks that would have been vulnerable to the economic events emerging in the 1980s. Commercial banking today is a slimmer and stronger industry. Unit banking laws created sheltered local banking markets fostering the survival of many more banks than would exist under more competitive conditions. What the multi-bank holding company has accomplished is to force a shake-out in local banking markets in the face of branch banking restrictions. A point not raised previously but possibly worth mentioning is the large increase in the number of new commercial banks chartered in the 1980s. It is fair to surmise that the environment for bank mergers and acquisitions is far from reaching the saturation point and that continuing high levels of bank merger and acquisition activity can be expected in coming years.

Commercial banking is a good example of the idea that markets are social constructions. The United States has a unique banking system compared with other advanced industrial nations. In other nations, the banking system is highly centralized with a few large banks dominating the industry, while the United States has a highly decentralized banking system. The dual state/federal banking system of the United States arose in response to the unique politics associated with the political ideology of states' rights. The political dynamics are still at play today as evidenced by the fact that over half of the commercial banks in the country are not members of the Federal Reserve and by the fact that federal banking laws still provide autonomy to state bank regulatory agencies. The political reality of bank regulation is buttressed by strong public opinion against impersonal banking practices. This is not surprising for it has long been observed that informal institutionalized practices lay at the root of formal institutional arrangements (Homans 1974; Nee and Ingram 1996). It will be interesting to see what the future holds for locally controlled banks, but if the results of this study are any indication, it is safe to predict that locally controlled banks will be with us for a long time to come.

In conclusion, three short-comings of this analysis are the lack of financial data on the parent bank holding companies, lack of data on events occurring after 1991, and lack of financial data for banks on years beyond 1988. Definitive conclusions regarding the financial performance of bank holding companies is impossible without financial information on subsidiaries of bank holding companies other than commercial banks. Haveman's (1992, 1993) studies of California savings and loan banks demonstrates the differential effects of financial product diversification strategies on the financial performance of individual savings and loan banks. Haveman's results support the findings of Rumelt (1974) that savings and loans which diversify financial product offerings along lines closely associated with prior services out-perform savings and loans which diversify into a wider range of services. Also, Kaufman and Mote (1994) attribute the strong financial performance of commercial banks in the 1990s to their ability to replace weak performing on-balance sheet services (traditional loans) with stronger income producing off-balance sheet activities such as mortgage bundling, investment services, and insurance services. Off-balance sheet services generate fees for services such as refinancing, credit cards, letters of credit, etc. Traditional on-balance sheet services generate income from interest on loans and investments. What is the role of bank holding company subsidiaries in financial product diversification and fee generated income flows? Answers to these questions would provide valuable information regarding the financial performance of bank holding companies. This type of analysis would be particularly revealing regarding the long-term persistence of one-bank holding companies.

Interpretation of Differential Equation Models

In this appendix, different interpretations of differential equation models are discussed with the intention of justifying the interpretation of the differential equation models in Chapter 5. The need for this discussion is due to the fact that differential equation models have been variously interpreted in terms of negative feedback systems (Coleman 1968), system stability or resistance to change (Nielsen and Rosenfeld 1981), and as partial adjustment models (Tuma and Hannan 1984). I maintain that these substantive interpretations are non-contradictory and consistent with the mathematical properties of the first order, partial differential equation models being considered. The differences in interpretation arise from the research context to which the models have been applied. The dynamic properties of differential equations have only recently been applied to social science research problems and additional interpretations may emerge in the future.

Confusion over the interpretation of differential equations exists because differential equations estimate instantaneous rates of change in the dependent variable which is an unobservable entity and cannot be estimated directly. Therefore, the estimation of differential equation models involves two steps. First, the integral equation form is estimated with the observed values of the dependent, lagged dependent, and independent variables. Second, transform the estimated parameters of the integral equation model to recover the unobserved, dynamic parameters of the underlying differential equation model.

In this appendix, I first present the differential equation model and then examine the three substantive interpretations of the differential equation model that are most commonly used by researchers. I conclude with a description of the method for transforming the estimated parameters of the integral equation into the dynamic parameters of the underlying differential equation model. The dynamic parameters consist of the rate of adjustment parameter which is derived from the coefficient of the lagged dependent variable and the long-term, target or equilibrium parameters which are derived from the coefficients of the explanatory variables.

If social processes are static over time then the system is in a steady or equilibrium state, and cross-sectional analysis is sufficient to explore causal relationships. However, dynamic social processes are often the case, and cross-sectional designs are unable to depict the structure of causal processes over time. It is to be expected that social systems undergoing change move from one equilibrium state to another. The analysis of movement from one steady state to another is central to the study of dynamic social processes and justifies the modeling of dynamic social processes with differential equations. If time changing social processes are expected to be moving toward some target or steady state over time then differential equation models are appropriate. The substantive parameters estimated by differential equations are the rate of change (the adjustment parameter derived from the lagged dependent variable) and influence on the long-term target or steady state level of the dependent variable by the explanatory variables.

First order, linear differential equations take the form

$$dy(t)/dt = cy(t) + b'x, \qquad (1)$$

where $y(t)$ is a lagged value of the dependent variable $y(t)$, c is the rate of change toward or away from a steady state. and $b'x$ are the effects of the explanatory variables. The sign and magnitude of rate of change parameter c is substantively important. A positive c indicates movement away from a steady state value and a negative c indicates movement toward a steady state value. In most sociological contexts, a negative c is expected since social systems are composed of relatively stable patterns of social behavior. The magnitude of c reflects the speed of movement toward or away from a steady state and in well-behaved systems the value of c will range between 0 and 1. A large value of c (close to 1) represents rapid movement and a small value of c (close to zero) indicates slow movement in each of the time periods analyzed. If the value of c is 0 then no change is occurring over the time period, and if the value of c is 1 then change is instantaneous.

The interpretation of coefficients for the effects of explanatory variables in dynamic models is different from the interpretation of static, cross-sectional models. Setting the right hand side of equation 1 equal to zero and solving for y^e provides the condition that holds when the system is in equilibrium.

$$y^e = -(1/c)b'x. \tag{2}$$

Note that the effects of the explanatory variables are composites of both b and c since dynamic models are explicitly modeling the behavior of systems over time.

Following Coleman (1968), Nielsen and Rosenfeld (1981), and Tuma and Hannan (1984) there are three basic substantive frameworks for interpreting linear differential equations taking the form of equations 1 and 2. The first interpretation focuses on system stability and is couched in terms of negative feedback. The concept of negative feedback is analogous to the concept of regression toward the mean. It is often observed when taking repeated measurements of the same individual over time that when the first observation is far from the mean then the second observation is closer to the mean. This interpretation assumes that the mean represents an equilibrium or criterion towards which the behavior of the individual is moving over time. In other words, negative feedback is manifest as regression toward some limiting value such as the mean.

Social processes or behaviors which display the tendency to move toward a limiting value can be characterized as stable, whereas, those that do not are unstable. The presence or absence of negative feedback in a social system is denoted by the sign of parameter c in equation 1, and the behavior of the system is represented by the sign of c in combination with the initial value of y $[y(t_0)]$. There are four general time paths which a system can follow, two representing stable systems and two representing unstable systems. When the sign of c is negative, negative feedback occurs and produces a stable system. If the sign of c is negative and the value $y(t_0)$ is above y^e, then $y(t)$ declines over time to y^e. If the sign of c is negative and the value of $y(t_0)$ is below y_e, then $y(t)$ increases over time to y^e. When the sign of c is positive, no negative feedback occurs and the system continuously moves away from equilibrium. If the sign of c is positive and the value of $y(t_0)$ begins above y^e, then the value of $y(t)$ grows indefinitely away from y^e. If the sign of c is positive and the value of $y(t_0)$ is below y^e, then the value of $y(t)$ decays to zero.

The second substantive interpretation of linear differential equations relates to the tendency of social systems to adjust in increments rather than fully to changing social conditions. For example, fertility rates in the United States over the twentieth century have adjusted in increments to the changing occupational role of women as they have increasingly moved from the home to the work place. The partial adjustment of social systems to changing social conditions in the short run is due to the effects of constraints on action imposed by institutions, norms, environmental uncertainty, opposition, etc. The partial adjustment model can be formally depicted by

$$dy(t)/dt = c[y^e(t) - y(t)], \tag{3}$$

where y^e denotes system targets or goals and the parameter c is expected to be negative and represents the rate of adjustment (per unit of time) of y to the difference between its current and target levels. When the value of c is negative and large, the social system adjusts rapidly toward its target. As the value of negative c approaches zero, the rate of adjustment decreases. The adjustment parameter is an important characteristic of social systems because it depends on specific structural qualities of the social system itself.

The target or goal of the system, y^e, is the level causal variables are impelling y over time. If it assumed that this dependence is linear and time stationary, then

$$y^e(t) = -(1/c)b'x(t). \tag{4}$$

By substituting equation 4 into equation 3, we get an equation in the form of equation 1,

$$dy(t)/dt = -c[-(1/c)b'x(t) - y(t)] = cy(t) + b'x(t). \tag{5}$$

This demonstrates that the negative feedback model can be understood as a partial adjustment model where the target or goal of the system depends linearly on a theoretically relevant set of explanatory variables.

The third interpretation of dynamic models is based on an assessment of the persistence of initial values of y over time, or in other words, the resistance of the social system to change (Nielsen and Rosenfeld 1981; Tuma and Hannan 1984:338). In other words, do the initial values of y remain static over time or do they change and at what rate? To demonstrate this, first transform equation 5 into an initial value form such that

$$y(t) = e^{c\Delta t}y_0 + [1 - e^{c\Delta t}]y^*, \qquad (6)$$

or

$$y(t) = \lambda y_0 + [1 - \lambda]y^e, \qquad (7)$$

where y_0 is the initial condition, $\lambda \equiv e^{c\Delta t}$, $\Delta t \equiv t - t_0$, and y^e is the target value toward which the system is moving.[1] The speed of adjustment, c, is

$$\lambda = e^{c\Delta t}$$

$$\ln \lambda = c\Delta t$$

$$c = -(\ln \lambda)/\Delta t$$

Notice that if $0 \le \lambda \le 1$, then c is negative. From these conditions it is evident that the value of y at any time t is a weighted average of the initial value of y and the target value y^e. Notice that the weight given the initial condition y_0 approaches zero as t approaches ∞ and also depends on the speed of adjustment. For large values of c, the effects of the initial condition are short-lived which means that y(t) deviates from the initial value y_0 which signifies a system undergoing relatively rapid change. For values of c close to zero, the effect of the initial condition endures and the value of y(t) remains close to the initial value which signifies a relatively static system. To reach these results it is important to assume that enough time has elapsed for the system to reach a steady state for with large values of t the value of $e^{c\Delta t}$ approaches zero in equations 6 and 7.

In conclusion, I present the integral equation form of the dynamic model which includes time varying explanatory variables and describe the transformations to recover the parameters of the underlying differential equation model.

$$y(t) = \lambda y(t_{t-1}) + \beta_1 x(t_{t-1}) + \beta_2 \Delta x(t), \qquad (8)$$

where $\lambda \equiv e^{c\Delta t}$, $\beta_1 \equiv (e^{c\Delta t}-1/c)b$, $\beta_2 \equiv [(\lambda-1-\ln \lambda)/(c^2\Delta t)]b$, $y(t-1)$ is the lagged endogenous variable, $x(t_{t-1})$ is the value of an explanatory variable at the beginning of each period, and $\Delta x(t)$, is the change in the value of the same explanatory variables from t-1 to t for each of the time periods. The parameters of the underlying differential equation (the dynamic model) can be recovered from the integral form of the equation with simple algebraic manipulations

$$c = \ln \lambda / \Delta t;$$

$$b^{(1)} = (c / \lambda - 1)\beta_1;$$

$$b^{(2)} = [(c^2\Delta t)/(\lambda - 1 - \ln \lambda)]\beta_2.$$

The two estimates of b have the same asymptotic expected value, however, it is often the case that in empirical applications the two values differ. It is suggested that the final estimator of b be estimated by taking a weighted linear combination of $b^{(1)}$ and $b^{(2)}$.

$$b = pb^{(1)} + (1-p)b^{(2)},$$

where $0 \le p \le 1$. Usually a value of .5 is chosen for p (Hannan and Freeman 1984:427-28). Note, that significance tests of the parameter estimates for $b^{(1)}$ and $b^{(2)}$ are commonly used to determine the statistical significance of the transformed, dynamic estimates of the explanatory variables which is an unproved assumption and may be inaccurate. It is the estimated parameters (c, b) of the dynamic model that are of interest in analyzing the stability or change in social systems over time.

I have repeatedly used the terms equilibrium, goal, target. However, one of the compelling rationales for the use of the partial adjustment model for empirical analysis is its flexibility for testing interesting hypotheses from a variety of theoretical perspectives. My interest is in adaptive decision-making processes, therefore, I employ the notion of goals and targets, but this is not to imply that this is the only theoretical interpretation of the level toward which causal forces are pushing y.

References

Alchian, Armen A. 1950. Uncertainty, evolution and economic theory. Journal of Political Economy 58:211-21.

Austin, Douglas V. 1989. Inside the Boardroom: How to be an Effective Bank Director. Homewood, IL: Dow Jones-Irwin.

Bank Holding Company Act. 1956. 70 Stat. 133, 12 U.S.C. 1972.

Bank Merger Act. 1966. 80 Stat. 7, 12 U.S.C. 1828.

Berger, Allen N. and David B. Humphrey. 1990. The dominance of inefficiencies over scale and product mix economies in banking. Finance and Economics Discussion Series 107. Board of Governors of the Federal Reserve System.

Blossfeld, Hans-Peter, Alfred Hamerle and Karl Ulrich Mayer. 1989. Event History Analysis: Statistical Theory and Application in the Social Sciences. Hillsdale, NJ: Lawrence Erlbaum Associates, Publishers.

Boyd, John H. and Stanley L. Graham. 1993. Investigating the banking consolidation trend. In Readings for the Economics of Money, Banking, and Financial Markets, eds. James W. Eaton and Frederic S. Mishkin. New York: HarperCollins Publishers, Inc.

Brint, Steven and Jerome Karabel. 1991. Institutional origins and transformations: the case of american community colleges. In The New Institutionalism in Organizational Analysis, eds. Walter W. Powell and Paul J. DiMaggio, pp. 337-60. Chicago: The University of Chicago Press.

Brown, Donald M. 1983. The effect of state banking laws on holding company banks. Federal Reserve Bank of St. Louis August/September(1983):26-35.

Burns, Arthur F. 1988. The Ongoing Revolution in American Banking. Washington, DC: American Enterprise Institute for Public Policy Research.

Caves, Richard E. 1992. American Industry: Structure, Conduct and Performance, 7th ed. Englewood Cliffs, NJ: Prentice-Hall.

Chandler, Alfred D. Jr. 1962. Strategy and Structure. New York: Doubleday & Company.

————. 1977. The Visible Hand: The Managerial Revolution in American Business. Cambridge, MA: The Belknap Press of Harvard University Press.

Clark, Jeffrey A. 1988. Economies of scale and scope at depository financial institutions: a review of the literature. Economic Review 73:16-33. Federal Reserve Bank of Kansas City.

Cole, David W. 1972. Return on equity model for banks. The Bankers Magazine 155(3):40-47.

Coleman, James S. 1968. The mathematical study of change. In Methodology in Social Research, eds. Hubert M. Blalock, Jr. and Ann B. Blalock, pp. 428-478. New York: McGraw-Hill Book Company.

————. 1990. Foundations of Social Theory. Cambridge, MA: The Belknap Press.

Cooper, Kerry and Donald R. Fraser. 1984. Banking Deregulation and the New Competition in Financial Services. Cambridge, MA: Ballinger Publishing.

Copeland, Thomas and J. Fred Weston. 1992. Financial Theory and Corporate Policy, 3rd Ed. Reading, MA: Addison-Wesley.

Davis, Gerald F., Kristina A. Diekmann, and Catherine H. Tinsley. 1994. The decline and fall of the conglomerate firm in the 1980s: the deinstitutionalization of an organizational form. American Sociological Review 59(4):547-570.

Davis, Gerald F. and Suzanne K. Stout. 1992. Organization theory and the market for corporate control: a dynamic analysis of the characteristics of large takeover targets, 1980-1990. Administrative Science Quarterly 37:(605-633.

Delacroix, Jacques, and Glenn R. Carroll. 1983. Organizational foundings: an ecological study of the newspaper industries of argentina and ireland. Administrative Science Quarterly 28:274-91.

Delacroix, Jacques, Anand Swaminathan, and Michael E. Solt. 1989. Density dependence versus population dynamics: an ecological study of failings in the california wine industry. American Sociological Review 54:245-62. Department of Justice. 1968. Merger Guidelines. Department of Justice Publications (May 30, 1968).

DiMaggio, Paul J. 1988. Interest and agency in institutional theory. In Institutional Patterns and Organizations: Culture and Environment, ed. Lynn G. Zucker. Cambridge, MA: Ballinger.

DiMaggio, Paul J. and Walter W. Powell. 1991. The iron cage revisited: institutional isomorphism and collective rationality. In The New Institutionalism in Organizational Analysis, eds. Walter W. Powell and Paul J. DiMaggio. Chicago: The University of Chicago Press.

Eccles, George S. 1982. The Politics of Banking, ed. Sidney Hyman. Salt Lake City: The University of Utah School of Business.

Eisenbeis, Robert A. 1987. Eroding market imperfections: implications for financial intermediaries, the payments system, and regulatory reform. In Restructuring the Financial System. A symposium sponsored by the Federal Reserve Bank of Kansas City: Jackson Hole, Wyoming August 20-22, 1987.

Fisher, Gerald C. 1961. Bank Holding Companies. New York: Columbia University Press.

Fligstein, Neil. 1985. The spread of the multidivisional form among large firms, 1919-1979. American Sociological Review 50:377-391.

―――. 1990. The Transformation of Corporate Control. Cambridge, MA: Harvard University Press.

―――. 1991. The structural transformation of American industry: an institutional account of the causes of diversification in the largest firms, 1919-1979. In The New Institutionalism in Organizational Analysis, eds. Walter W. Powell and Paul J. DiMaggio. Chicago: The University of Chicago Press.

―――. 1996. A political-cultural approach to market institutions. American Sociological Review 61:656-673.

Frank, Robert H. 1991. Microeconomics and Behavior. New York: McGraw-Hill, Inc.

Friedman, Debra and Michael Hechter. 1988. The contribution of rational choice theory to macrosociological research. Sociological Theory 6(2):201-218.

Friedman, Milton and Anna Jacobson Schwartz. 1963. A Monetary History of the United States, 1867-1960. Princeton, NJ: Princeton University Press.

Fuller, Wayne A. and George E. Battese. 1974. Estimation of linear models with crossed-error structure. Journal of Econometrics 2:67-78.

Greene, William H. 1990. Econometric Analysis. New York: MacMillan Publishing Company.

Gujarati, Damodar N. 1988. Basic Econometrics, 2nd Ed. New York: McGraw-Hill, Inc.

Hammond, Bray. 1957. Banks and Politics in America: from the Revolution to the Civil War. Princeton, NJ: Princeton University Press.

Hannan, Michael T. and Glenn R. Carroll. 1992. Dynamics of Organizational Populations: Density, Legitimation, and Competition. New York: Oxford University Press.

Hannan, Michael T. and John Freeman. 1977. The population ecology of organizations. American Journal of Sociology 82:929-64.

―――. 1989. Organizational Ecology. Cambridge, MA: Harvard University Press.

Haveman, Heather A. 1992. Between a rock and a hard place: organizational change and performance under conditions of fundamental environmental transformation. Administrative Science Quarterly 37:48-75.

————. 1993. Organizational size and change: diversification in the savings and loan industry after deregulation. Administrative Science Quarterly 38:20-50.

Hawawini, Gabriel A. and Itzhak Swary. 1990. Mergers and Acquisitions in the U.S. Banking Industry: Evidence from the Capital Markets. Amsterdam: Elsevier Science Publishers.

Homans, George C. 1974. Social Behavior: Its Elementary Forms, 2nd Ed.. New York: Harcourt Brace Jovanovic.

Huertas, Thomas F. 1987. Redesigning regulation: the future of finance in the united states. In Restructuring the Financial System. A symposium sponsored by the Federal Reserve Bank of Kansas City: Jackson Hole, Wyoming August 20-22, 1987.

Humphrey, David B. 1990. Why do estimates of bank scale economies differ? Economic Review 76:38-50. Federal Reserve Bank of Richmond.

Independent Bankers Association of America. 1978. Independent Banking Serves America. Sauk Centre, MN: The Independent Bankers Association of America.

Johnson, Frank P. and Richard D. Johnson. 1985. Commercial Bank Management. Chicago: Dryden Press.

Johnston, J. 1984. Econometric Methods, 3rd Ed. New York: McGraw-Hill.

Kalbfleisch, John D. and Ross L. Prentice. 1980. The Statistical Analysis of Failure Time Data. New York: John Wiley and Sons.

Kaufman, George G. 1992. The U.S. Financial System: Money, Markets, and Institutions, 5th Ed. Englewood Cliffs, NJ: Prentice Hall, Inc.

Kaufman, George G. and Larry R. Mote. 1994. Is banking a declining industry? a historical perspective. Economic Perspectives 18(3):2-21.

Koch, Timothy W. 1992. Bank Management, 2nd. Ed. Fort Worth, TX: Dryden Press.

Lenski, Gerhard E. 1993. Power and distributive systems. In Power in Modern Societies, eds. Marvin E. Olsen and Martin N. Marger, pp. 59-67. Boulder, CO: Westview Press.

Marris, Robin. 1964. The Economic Theory of Managerial Capitalism. Glencoe, IL: Free Press.

Meyer, John W. and Brian Rowan. 1977. Institutionalized organizations: formal structure as myth and ceremony. American Journal of Sociology 83:340-363.

Mishkin, Frederic S. 1992. The Economics of Money, Banking, and Financial Markets, 3rd Ed. New York: HarperCollins Publishers Inc.

Mueller, Dennis C. 1986. Profits in the Long Run. London: Cambridge University Press.

Nee, Victor. 1991. Social Exchange and Political Process in Maoist China. New York: Garland Publishing.

Nee, Victor and Paul Ingram. (forthcoming) Embeddedness and beyond: institutions, exchange and social structure. In The New Institutionalism in Sociology, eds. Victor Nee and Mary C. Brinton.

Nee, Victor and Peng Lian. 1994. Sleeping with the enemy: a dynamic model of declining political commitment in state socialism. Theory and Society 23:253-96.

Nielsen, Francois and Rachel A. Rosenfeld. 1981. Substantive interpretations of differential equation models. American Sociological Review 46:159-174.

North, Douglass C. 1981. Structure and Change in Economic History. New York: W. W. Norton & Company.

————. 1990. Institutions, Institutional Change and Economic Performance. Cambridge: Cambridge University Press.

Olson, Mancur. 1965. The Logic of Collective Action: Public Goods and the Theory of Groups. Cambridge, MA: Harvard University Press.

Palmer, Donald, Brad M. Barber, Xueguang Zhou, and Yasemin Soysal. 1995. The acquisition of large U.S. corporations in the 1960s. American Sociological Review 60(4):469-99.

Palmer, Donald, Roger Friedland, P. Devereaux Jennings, and Melanie Powers. 1987. The economics and politics of structure: the multidivisional form and the large U.S. corporation. Administrative Science Quarterly 32:25-48).

Palmer, Donald, P. Devereaux Jennings, and Xueguang Zhou. 1993. Late adoption of the multidivisional form by large U.S. corporations: institutional, political, and economic accounts. Administrative Science Quarterly 38:100-31.

Polanyi, Karl. 1944. The Great Transformation: The Political and Economic Origins of Our Time. Boston: Beacon Press.

Powell, Walter W. 1988. Institutional effects on organizational structure and performance. In Institutional Patterns and Organization, ed. Lynn Zucker, 115-136. Cambridge, MA: Ballinger.

Rose, Peter S. 1988. Bank Mergers in a Deregulated Environment: Scrutinizing the Promises, Avoiding the Pitfalls. Rolling Meadows, Il: Bank Administration Institute.

Rumelt, Richard P. 1974. Strategy, Structure, and Economic Performance. Boston, MA: Harvard Business School.

Simon, Herbert A. 1954. Some strategic considerations in the construction of social science models. In Mathematical Thinking in the Social Sciences, ed. Paul Lazarsfeld. Glencoe, IL: The Free Press.

————. 1958. The role of expectations in an adaptive or behavioristic model. In Expectations, Uncertainty, and Business Behavior, ed. M. J. Bowsman, pp. 49-58. New York: Social Science Research Council.

————. 1976. Administrative Behavior: A Study of Decision-Making Processes in Administrative Organization, 3rd ed. New York: The Free Press.

Starr, Paul. 1982. The Social Transformation of American Medicine. New York: Basic Books.

Stinchcombe, Arthur L. 1965. Social structure and organizations. In Handbook of Organizations, pp. 142-93, ed. James G. March. Chicago: Rand McNally.

Strang, David and Ellen M. Bradburn. 1993. Theorizing legitimacy or legitimating theory? competing institutional accounts of hmo policy, 1970-1989. Unpublished paper presented at the 1993 meetings of the American Sociological Association, Miami.

Swary, Itzhak. 1980. Capital Adequacy Requirements and Bank Holding Companies. Ann Arbor, MI: University Microfilms International.

Torres, David L. 1988. Professionalism, variation, and organizational survival. American Sociological Review 53:380-94.

Tuma, Nancy Brandon and Michael T. Hannan. 1984. Social Dynamics: Models and Methods. Orlando, FL: Academic Press, Inc.

Weber, Max. 1978. Economy and Society. Berkeley: University of California Press.

Williamson, Oliver. 1975. Markets and Hierarchies: Analysis and Antitrust Implications. New York: The Free Press.

————. 1985. The Economic Institutions of Capitalism. New York: The Free Press.

Index